SOLD

SOLD

*A Story of
Modern-Day Slavery*

Zana Muhsen
with
Andrew Crofts

BCA

LONDON NEW YORK SYDNEY TORONTO

First published in Great Britain by Futura in 1991
This edition published 1994
by BCA by arrangement with
Little, Brown and Company
Copyright © 1991 by Zana Muhsen and Andrew Crofts

First reprint 1994

CN 3399

A CIP catalogue record for this book
is available from the British Library.

Photoset in North Wales by
Derek Doyle & Associates, Mold, Clwyd
Printed in England by Clays Ltd, St Ives plc

Little, Brown and Company (UK) Limited

Preface

When Zana Muhsen first escaped from the Yemen, the news was on front pages all over the world. The media was queuing up to buy her story, but Zana wasn't ready to talk. She needed time to reflect and to put her ordeal into perspective. After a year, when the media attention had calmed down, she decided it was time to tell her story and she looked for a writer to help her. She chose to talk to Andrew Crofts, an author, journalist and travel writer who also ghostwrites books for people with stories to tell, from business tycoons to Hollywood filmstars, and ordinary people caught up in extraordinary events. Together they relived the painful, thirteen year nightmare, to produce a true picture of Zana's story.

When the book was first published in Britain there were legal difficulties about publicizing it. But in France it was the bestselling non-fiction book of 1992. It topped the charts in every country from Sweden to Turkey, and has been translated into eighteen languages so far. Now the legal difficulties are over and British readers will be able to share in the incredible, heart-wrenching story which has had all of Europe talking.

Introduction

This is a story of a terrible clash between some of the most primitive elements which still survive in our modern world, and some of the most sophisticated people on earth. It centres on two young schoolgirls from Birmingham, sisters whose tragic fate has caused governments to fall out, families to split and two cultures to crash headlong into one another.

Zana Muhsen was taken from her home and dragged first to a world where peasants scratch a bare living from rocky soil, and then to another where individuals control media conglomerates, charter private aeroplanes in order to trot the globe and have access to the palaces and powerhouses of Western Europe. This could be a tale from *The Arabian Nights*, except that it is happening now, and it turned out to be a living nightmare, not a dream at all.

The Yemen is one of the poorest nations on earth, with much of its population still living as they have done for the last thousand years. Most of the able-bodied men get jobs abroad in order to send home money for food, while their women stay in their villages, locked behind their veils, looking after their families with back-breaking toil and no respite this side of the grave.

It is a fierce, dangerous, primitive world, where the men are completely dominant and the women have to accept their lot in life, whether it is to be married off at the age of nine to a boy they hardly know, to walk a mile to a well every day of their lives to bring water back to their homes, or to plant and harvest crops in barren soil, with little more than a hand trowel, year after year.

When two Birmingham girls, Nadia and Zana Muhsen, are sent out to the Yemen by their father for a holiday, they are told to expect an adventure. They are told to expect fabulous beaches, bareback riding and camel racing. Instead they find they have been married off, at fourteen and fifteen, to boys in the tribal villages of the Mokbana region. In this medieval world the women have virtually no rights and absolutely no control over their lives. They are completely within the power of the men in their families. The men are a law unto themselves. Strangers who venture into the mountains asking questions, simply disappear.

Nadia and Zana were not the first girls from countries like Britain and America to be tricked into marriages and into lifetimes of servitude in the Yemen, but Zana was the first to escape, with the help of her mother and the British media.

It took her mother six years to find the girls, hidden away in the mountains, and another two years to find a way for Zana to get out. But neither Zana nor her mother ever gave up hope or stopped fighting. Although Zana was forced outwardly to become a Yemeni wife, just as the men wanted her to be, she always dreamed of getting back to England and her family. She never allowed them to break her spirit, not with the endless work, the beating, the diseases, the mental cruelty, the rapes or the agonies of childbirth in the raw. In her eight years as an Arab peasant woman, Zana gained an unrivalled insight into how life is for women out there, and how life must have been for women in many other countries just a short time ago, before we took for granted things like running water, electricity, contraception, anaesthetics, equal rights and medical care.

Nadia is still a prisoner in the Mokbana, and in writing this book Zana hoped to show the men who imprison her sister just how much they are making her suffer by enforcing a lifestyle on her which seems natural to them but which inflicts such pain on the foreign girls who are not brought up to it.

Escaping from the Yemen herself was only half the battle. In trying to free her sister Zana has travelled all over the world, getting help from wherever she can to battle with the red tape and hypocrisy of the international diplomatic and political world. In France, through the success of the book, she won the support and friendship of some of the country's most influential people, who joined her to do battle with politicians and leaders at the highest levels, but the gulfs between the ways of the new world and those of the old have merely become wider.

This is the story of an ordinary girl with extraordinary courage and tenacity, who has refused to allow world leaders to say 'no' to her and who will never give in. A girl who expected to be a nursery nurse in Birmingham, and would never have believed that she would become a media star in Paris, at home on live television shows and befriended by the daughter of a President.

CHAPTER ONE

A Childhood in Birmingham

I must have been about seven. I was in the house, messing around with my sister Nadia. I remember hitting her and making her cry. My Mum came after me and I ran out the front door into Lincoln Street where we were living. I was half laughing and half frightened of what Mum would do if she caught me.

There was a van parked next to the pavement and I dodged round it into the road. The next thing I knew I was being lifted into the air by a passing car. I seemed to be flying for ages before I hit the ground with my knees and my head, everything was confusing after that, with people shouting and moving me around.

I remember the ambulance coming and taking me to hospital. I had stitches in my head, and my knees are still scarred today. That is my first vivid memory.

I don't remember anything much about my life before then, I certainly don't remember ever being unhappy. I enjoyed my life with my family.

There were a lot of us living in Lincoln Street. It was my Nan's house, and we had all moved in with her from Sparkbrook, where I had been born. As well as Dad and Mum, there were four of my Mum's brothers living with us as well – my uncles. These uncles weren't much older than me. They were more like brothers than uncles. Mum used to look after them at the time. She was the eldest of Nan's thirteen children, so she took over the running of the house as Nan grew older, looking after the brothers who hadn't left home, at the same time as looking after her own children.

Mum and Dad had two children before me, Leilah and Ahmed, but my Dad had taken them down to visit his family in Aden when I was just two, and they had stayed there with our grandparents. He told Mum they were just going for a visit, they were three and four, but they never came back. I found out later how upset my Mum had been about losing them, but I didn't know anything about it at the time. Mum was always quiet about things; as far as we were concerned they had just gone to live somewhere else, we never questioned why.

Apparently, when Dad took them down to Aden to visit his family, he was gone for nine months, never sending any word back to Mum. When he came back without Leilah and Ahmed Mum couldn't believe what had happened. He told her that it was the best thing for the kids to stay in Aden, they would have a better life with their grandparents than he and Mum could offer them in England.

'My father has a big, beautiful house in the village of Marais,' Dad told her. 'The children wanted to stay there.'

'How could they choose,' Mum asked him. 'They are just babies?' But he wouldn't listen.

She tried writing to the Foreign Office and the Home Office, but they wrote back saying that Leilah and Ahmed were of dual nationality, British by their mother and Yemeni by their father, and so now they were in Aden they were considered Yemeni citizens.

She kept writing to people for two years, but no-one would help, and then she fell pregnant again and had to get on with her life in England. She told herself that it must be true that Leilah and Ahmed had a better life out there with their grandfather, and we never talked about them much as we were growing up.

Nadia and I had two younger sisters, Ashia and Tina,

and a baby brother called Mo. We were all living together in Lincoln Street.

Although I had run out the front door on the day of the accident, there was actually quite a big garden out the back of the house, where we used to breed pigeons. There were always a lot of people around, most of them relations on Mum's side. Dad didn't have any of his relations living in England, so we never got to hear much about his family or his past, apart from things which he chose to tell us. He was working for British Steel then, and doing other little jobs on the side to earn a bit more. Money must have been tight for Mum with so many of us to feed, but I don't remember having to go without anything. After Nan died everyone started to move out of Lincoln Street. My uncles went first, and then Mum, Dad, me and my brother and sisters moved to a house in Washwood Heath for a time. After a while Dad must have decided that he wanted to change his life. I think he may have been made redundant from British Steel and decided he wanted to just work for himself.

I was happy when we moved to Sparkbrook. I was about ten and I loved the area the moment I saw it. My Dad had swapped our house with a Turkish friend of his for a fish and chip shop on the Stratford Road, and we were all going to live above the café. It was a very ordinary street, full of shops and houses, but it seemed friendly and I felt comfortable there immediately. I wanted to stay forever.

We arrived ahead of the big removal van and Mum told me that this was the area where Nadia and I had been born. Once we had moved our belongings in we all started cleaning out the café and mopping the floors to get ready for opening. Nadia and I always loved helping Mum with the work. Dad made a few alterations to the shop, and re-opened it about a week later.

Dad didn't take much notice of us girls when we were small. He was out all day working, and when he came in

3

at night he was usually with his friends, talking Arabic. It wasn't until we got to secondary school that he began to act differently from everyone else's fathers. In his eyes we were beginning to turn into women, and it seemed to him that we were surrounded by dangerous temptations. He started to become very strict with us.

By the time Nadia and I were twelve or thirteen he was watching us all the time. Every time I wanted to go out I had to make up stories for him. I would tell him I was going to my uncle's to babysit whenever I wanted to go round to a friend's house or out to a party or a disco. There was a Family Association Centre just round the corner from the café which held discos each week. I loved going round there with my friends. If my uncle saw Dad he would stick up for me and say I was round at his house. Mum knew what we were doing as well, but she kept quiet. Perhaps she could understand better than us why he became so angry with us, but she didn't say anything.

He didn't like us wearing skirts that showed our legs, even though they came down to our knees. He didn't like the people I was hanging round with, or the Sparkbrook area because of the men he believed were walking around the streets after dark. Most of all he hated black people. All his Arab friends felt the same way. There were a lot of black boys down at the Centre and he knew I was friendly with them. He even hated the reggae and soul music which I listened to because it was mainly by black artists. I used to ask Mum, 'What's he got against black people?' She'd say, 'I don't know, ask him,' but I never had the guts to ask a question like that. He used to say that where he came from black people were slaves, and that was how things should be.

I was too young then to understand about black history. Later I was to discover just how much the Ethiopians had done towards building Egypt and the other Arab countries, and that the Arabs originally came out of Africa.

I could never understand why he felt like that because I had been brought up amongst people of all different races, and I never thought of them as different. I liked all the people I went to St Albans Church of England School with – I always had a great time with all my friends whatever colour they were. Dad didn't mind me talking to all the boys and men who came into the café as customers, but if he saw me talking to a man outside, either black or white, he would start acting strangely, questioning me about who they were even though he knew them, and warning me not to let him catch me talking to them again. Nadia had exactly the same problems with him.

He was moody sometimes, and there were times, like when he wouldn't even let me go round to my uncle's, when I used to think I really hated him. My friends seemed to be able to go out every night. Their dads would tell them to be in by nine, or whatever, but at least they were able to go out. I wasn't allowed out of the house again after getting in from school unless I made up a story for him. I wasn't going to let him ruin my life. By the time I was fifteen I used to sneak out anyway, whatever he said, and leave my Mum to explain where I was. I knew that it would mean getting a smack or a telling off when I got in but it was worth it. He never hit me hard, it was mostly telling off. Whenever I came in I would just go straight to my bedroom without speaking to him if possible. Because he didn't trust us he sometimes used to follow us when we went out, to make sure that we were going where we said. If he lost sight of us he would challenge us when we got home, demanding to know where we had been, what we had been doing, who we had been seeing. I learnt to just keep denying everything.

I was learning to take no notice of him, and that made him all the angrier. I didn't believe any of the awful things which he said would happen to us if we went out on our own in the evenings. I never felt frightened on the street, I always felt safe. This was my area, I knew everyone who passed by, I knew what I was doing. Even if we came in at six in the evening he would demand to know where we'd been. I would say we had been at school, although we had usually been to the Family Centre and the park with our friends. We never wanted to stay in at that age. Mum always kept very quiet, but I knew that she used to stick up for us when we weren't around.

Not that we went out all the time. Most evenings Nadia and I would stay in and help Mum in the café. She had worked before, but she hadn't run a café. It was hard work but we all enjoyed it. There were always lots of people around. Upstairs, above the shop, we had two living rooms and three bedrooms. My sisters and I all shared a bedroom at the top of the house. We fought a lot, just like any sisters, but we all got on well. Ashia was younger than Nadia and me and she used to follow us everywhere. I thought she was too young and I used to try to get her to go away. She would blackmail me to let her hang around, threatening to tell Dad what we were up to if I didn't. Nadia and I were the closest. I always wanted to be with her. I felt I needed to look after her, she was the most important person in my life.

Although Nadia and I were together most of the time, we had different groups of friends. Nadia was a year behind me in school and she was more of a tom-boy than me. Even if we went to the park together she would be on the football field or climbing trees with her friends while I'd be in the Centre playing table tennis or pool, or reading a book. We had different interests, but we always knew where the other one was. Nadia's friends got into trouble more than mine did, but it was always for trivial things like fighting in the street, never anything serious.

There was always plenty to do at the Centre. We used to spend most of our time painting things for the children's activities, making pictures and new things to go on the boards. The Centre was for all age groups, and we liked helping the staff with the younger kids. They used to hold competitions for things like fancy dress. I remember we made a massive Christmas card for some-one to wear in one contest, and it won a prize of two pounds. I half wanted to wear the costume myself but I was too embarrassed, I thought I was getting too old for that sort of thing really.

The café seemed to do quite well. We did take-away fish and chips as well as having some tables for people to sit at. There was a pool table in there, which the local lads used all the time, and coin machines. There always seemed to be customers around. By helping Mum to serve them, Nadia and I got to know everyone in the area. It was all very friendly and we never had any trouble.

Nadia and I were both very average at school. Nadia used to get into trouble a bit for messing around in the classroom with her friends, and the teachers always said I was too 'talkative' in my end of term reports. I was good at English, I enjoyed reading, writing and spelling. The teacher was always getting me to stand up and read out loud in the classroom and I enjoyed that.

I always had books which I was reading for myself as well. I carried Mills and Boon romances around with me in my handbag wherever I went. I used to take them into the park with me. Once I'd started them I couldn't put them down. Some weekends I would just go to the park on my own, sit on a swing all day and read by myself, losing myself in the stories. I used to cry at the ends of the sad ones. I've always been emotional. I still cry at sad stories on the television or in magazines.

When I got a copy of *Roots*, about the slaves being taken from their homes in Africa to the plantations in the American South, I read it over and over again. I think I must have read it six times in all. I had no way of knowing how relevant it would be to my own life later on.

One Saturday morning in 1979 Mum, Nadia and I went up

town to do some shopping. We were in a busy market, browsing around the stalls looking at the racks of dresses and the barrows laid out with everything from handbags to records. Nadia was standing at a jewellery stall, looking at what they had. She saw a ring she liked, picked it up and turned to Mum.

'Mum,' she called out, 'will you buy me this?'

The ring was ninety pence. As Mum went over to her the man from behind the stall ran out and grabbed Nadia, accusing her of trying to run off with the ring without paying. Everyone started shouting and the stallholder called the police and accused Nadia of stealing. We all had to go to court and my Mum and I gave evidence. There were no other witnesses. We explained what had happened, but the stallholder still swore that Nadia was stealing, and the court believed him. My Mum was fined and Nadia was put on probation, with a social worker assigned to her. None of us had ever been in any trouble and it upset us badly because we all knew that there was no way Nadia intended to take the ring.

What we didn't realise was how badly Dad had taken it. He didn't come to the court with us, or offer to help out in any way, but to his Arab friends he talked about the shame of having his family name dragged into the courts, and his daughter branded as a thief. It seemed to confirm his fears that we were in moral danger and needed to be brought back onto the 'straight and narrow' path and taught how to behave like good Arab women.

Although Dad made a fuss about Nadia being branded a thief, I later found out that his family believed he was a thief and a cheat himself. When I met them later in the Yemen they told me he had stolen his stepmother's gold in order to get the money to come to England.

Back in the late sixties Mum received a telegram from Dad from Winson Green Prison, asking her to go to one of his friends to get some money which he owed the courts. Mum had realised he had gone to court in the morning to see them about the money he owed them, but she had no idea that they had imprisoned him until the evening telegram.

She did as he asked and his friend paid up to free him, but every week after that Mum had to go to the courts to pay fines for things like motoring offences and non-payment of rates. She even had to go to pay the bailiffs for him because he was too ashamed to face them himself.

CHAPTER TWO

A Father's Plot

Dad's Arab friends were always around the house from as far back as I can remember. They were all men, who would pop in to see him at all times of the day and night, and they always talked to one another in Arabic all the time. I got used to them when I was little and never took any notice of them. They never included women and girls in their conversations; it was as if we didn't exist for them.

One man in particular was around right from the time when we were babies, his name was Gowad. He and Dad were best friends, always talking and playing cards. I learnt the odd Arabic phrase like 'thank you' and 'would you like a cup of tea', but I never had any idea what they were talking about amongst themselves. I was never interested, it was grown-up men's talk, nothing that would affect me, as far as I knew.

In the evenings the men would often go off to the pub together, and Mum would stop in the café with us. We never had any idea what they were up to. Mum never seemed to mind the way he treated her, I suppose she was used to it. I think she thought my Dad was all right compared to some of the men her friends were with. She never complained about him to us, although I heard later from other people that she used to feel sad when she took us to the park on her own as kids, and saw other fathers taking an interest in their families. Although

10

Mum and Dad were together for nearly twenty years, and had seven children together, Dad never married her.

They first met when Mum was seventeen. Dad was from a village called Marais, outside the port city of Aden in South Yemen. He told her that he had run away to England when he was fifteen because he had been forced into an arranged marriage by his family and wanted to escape.

He would often go away for long periods at a time, like when he took Leilah and Ahmed down to Marais he was gone for nine months, leaving Mum on her own in a room in Birmingham. Most of his friends were like that, going home to the Yemen for a few months and then coming back to England for a while to work. A lot of them went to oil-rich places like Saudi Arabia and Kuwait to earn money as well. There isn't much work for men in the Yemen, so most of them have to travel abroad and send money back to their parents and wives. Most of them seem to like the lifestyle of moving around the world, it gives them freedom and allows them to behave as they please, knowing that the women are staying home, bringing up their children and looking after their houses and bits of land.

Just before I left school I got a part-time job cleaning offices. I would turn up at the offices after school with Lynette, my best friend from school, and they would tell us what to do. That gave me a bit of spare money for things like cigarettes and records. I always liked reggae and soul music, I still buy records all the time.

I started smoking one or two cigarettes a day, but I had to keep it secret from Dad. You could buy single cigarettes in the shops in those days, and I used to pinch them off Mum before I had enough money to buy my own. We had a toilet out in the back yard behind the café and I used to go out there to smoke. Mum came out to the toilet after me once and saw smoke and she warned me that Dad would kill me if he caught me.

I can't remember why I started smoking, but I do

remember that before I started people always used to compliment me on my brilliant white teeth. The cigarettes soon put a stop to that. I didn't start smoking really heavily until I left England.

Most of the time Dad didn't mind me seeing Lynette. Her parents had a shop in the Stratford Road, and I used to go down there and help them out whenever I could.

I never intended to keep going with the office cleaning job for long. I had only been doing it for two or three months when I heard about the holiday planned for us in the Yemen.

I actually wanted to train to be a nursery nurse. I really loved working with the kids at the Centre, and I had been taking childcare lessons at school. Every Wednesday we were allowed to choose a hobby which we really wanted to study. Some kids used to want to be librarians so they would go off to the libraries on Wednesdays. I went to the nurseries to look after the children and watch what the nurses used to do. It was like a course. I wanted to go to college and train to do it professionally. I had always liked looking after small children, I think I was mature for my age.

One evening Nadia, Ashia and I were round at the Centre. When we got back to the café it was about nine o'clock in the evening. We all went running upstairs into the living room and found a bunch of Arab guys sitting down with Mum and Dad. Dad's old friend Gowad was one of them.

Dad didn't seem cross that we were late for once. He introduced us to the others, which was unusual, and they all talked in English, including us in the conversation. The atmosphere was very friendly. There was a man there with his grown-up son. The man was called Abdul Khada, and his son was called Mohammed. I asked Mohammed how long he had been in England and he told me he had been here working in a factory for four years. Before that he had had a good job in Saudi Arabia, earning a lot of money. I guess he must have stayed in England to get his naturalisation papers, so that he could come and go as he pleased. That is what most of them do. They like to learn the English language because a second language sets them apart when they go back to the Yemen. Mohammed spoke English well and he seemed very nice. Abdul Khada was a short, plump man. He had a big moustache and curly hair and big eyes. He seemed to be a bad tempered man, but he was nice to me then.

Gowad had pictures of his family, particularly his son, which he was showing to us. We showed a polite interest, out of respect, but we didn't take much notice. Gowad was being particularly nice to Nadia. We all talked for a while, and eventually the other men left.

After they had gone Dad told Nadia that Gowad had offered to take her to the Yemen for a month's holiday, to visit our brother Ahmed and sister Leilah. He had often talked about how wonderful his home country was, and now he painted a picture which made it sound like one of those places where they make film commercials for Bounty chocolate bars. He talked about beautiful beaches fringed with palm trees, sunshine all the time and camel rides across the desert. He described the houses they all lived in on the cliffs overlooking the blue seas and clean sands, and talked of castles at the top of sand dunes. He said she would be staying on a farm and would be taught how to ride horses bareback.

It sounded so wonderful that Ashia and I said we wanted to go too. I also wasn't happy about Nadia going on her own, she seemed too young to travel all that way with strangers at fourteen, and she never went anywhere without me. I told Dad that I wanted to go with her. I was jealous of her getting such a wonderful holiday in a way, and I didn't want to be without her for six weeks, but I was also worried about her going on her own.

Dad listened to me and gave the impression that this was the first time he had thought of me going. He nodded wisely and said, 'We'll see'. He was obviously very

13

thoughtful about the idea.

He must have gone back to his friends then to discuss it, and a few days later he told me that Abdul Khada and his son Mohammed were going back to the Yemen a couple of weeks before Gowad, and they had kindly offered to do the same for me, taking me down to visit his family and then on with Nadia to stay with our Leilah and Ahmed for a holiday. I was very excited. It would be the first holiday I had ever had, and my first trip on an aeroplane. I thought I could have a little break, get a suntan, and then come back and get on with my childcare studies.

Although I wanted to travel on the same day as Nadia, I was scared I might get left behind if I didn't go when a ticket was offered, so I agreed to go on my own with Abdul Khada and Mohammed two weeks before Nadia.

Mum was very quiet, although she seemed happy for us that we were going to have a nice holiday. I remember asking her how I would manage without being able to speak Arabic, because I knew that Ahmed and Leilah both spoke it and didn't speak English. I knew because they used to send tapes to Dad, telling him how they were getting on, but they never spoke in English. He used to play the tapes to his friends, to show how happy his children were. Mum never talked about how she felt about those tapes. I think she found it hurt too much and since she felt there was nothing she could do she stayed out of it. I just assumed that if Dad said they were okay, then they must be.

If Nadia was to go to the Yemen, Mum was going to have to get permission for her to leave the country from her social worker. Mum thought that a break would do Nadia good because of all the stress which the court case had caused her, and she phoned to ask permission. They wouldn't give a reply there and then, they listened to her request and told her that she would have to wait for a reply. Nadia's social worker made a visit to the house and said they had checked on Gowad and that it would be all right for Nadia to go with him for a holiday. We were both so excited at the prospect of such an adventure, and quite scared.

CHAPTER THREE

Going Away

It was the end of June 1980 when we went away, a week before my sixteenth birthday and four months before Nadia's fifteenth.

The night before I was due to fly out some of my friends asked us both to go down to the Centre. Dad knew we were going and he didn't seem bothered. It didn't seem to matter to him what time we got in that night. I suppose we should have thought that was strange, but we were just happy to be free to please ourselves for the evening.

My friends came to meet me at the house, they were all giggling and whispering and having a good time about something. We all walked down to the Centre in a crowd and Ashia came with us. As I came through the door of the Centre I found the place full of balloons and people.

'What's going on?' I asked, looking around.

'It's a going-away party,' they said, 'for you and Nadia.'

I couldn't believe what they had done. There was a disco with a disc jockey and food and drinks and everything. It was a great night, the place was packed with everyone I knew, all wishing us luck and telling us how they envied us the chance we had to see a bit of the world and sample an exotic desert life. They all knew Dad, and they knew that he came from somewhere a long way away and very mysterious and beautiful.

16

One of the organisers at the Centre stood up on a platform and took the microphone to make a speech for us and said that everyone was to enjoy themselves. I started to cry at the thought of leaving them all. Even though I thought it would only be for six weeks, I had never been away from them at all until then, and it seemed like an age. We stayed dancing and talking until midnight.

Outside the party, in the quiet and dark of the Birmingham night, the men were preparing themselves for the trip. They had made all the arrangements and now they were waiting back at our house. As we danced and laughed and chattered, they sat above the cafe talking.

Eventually we left the party and walked home through the cool, empty night streets, still happy, but increasingly nervous about the adventures that lay in store.

There was a coach coming to pick us up at three in the morning, to take us to Heathrow Airport, down near London. When Nadia, Ashia and I got in after twelve we found Mum and Dad were both up and talking to Abdul Khada and his son Mohammed in the living room. Mum told us to go upstairs and get some sleep, promising to wake us when the coach arrived. I told her I wasn't tired. I was too excited to sleep. The men didn't take much notice of us.

All my friends had said they would come round to the house between one and two to say a last goodbye. I told them to come round the back and wait outside for me, because I knew Dad would go mad if he saw them.

The three men stayed in the front room. I could hear them talking in Arabic so I knew they wouldn't be coming out. Nadia and I sneaked down when we knew our friends were all congregating out the back, and we all stood around the back gate talking and giggling. One of my closest friends, Susan, started crying and saying 'Don't go, I don't want you to go.' I told her not to worry and said, 'I'll be back in a bit, I won't be long.' I felt very tearful myself at leaving them all behind, and nervous about travelling so far from the familiar things of my life.

'All right then,' Susan said, 'but make sure you write to me.'

In the early hours of the morning they all began to drift off home and Nadia and I went back inside. Nadia kissed me goodbye and went upstairs to bed. I was tense with excitement and I sat up with the three men who were playing cards in the front room, until the coach arrived just before three. Its engine was the only sound in the night and the men sprang up, leaving all the cards and money where they were. They seemed in such a rush to get going. The next time I saw Nadia she told me that when she and the other kids got up the next morning they found all the cards and money still lying around the table where the men had been playing. She told me they spent it all on sweets.

When we got outside the night had grown chilly and there were already some other people on board the coach, their faces illuminated in the interior lights, staring out at us, wide-eyed with a mixture of tiredness and excitement. Mum and Dad were both coming to the airport to see the men and me off. I didn't sleep at all on the drive down, I just stared out of the window into the darkness, and imagined what it was going to be like in the Yemen.

It was just getting light by the time we arrived at Heathrow but the plane wasn't due to leave until ten o'clock. The airport was already beginning to bristle with life, as early morning planes took off and businessmen rushed to catch them.

We were hungry and there were some delicious cooking smells coming from somewhere, so we all went into the terminal restaurant to get some breakfast. Abdul Khada was being very kind and generous towards me, buying me whatever I wanted, anxious that I should be comfortable and happy. I trusted him completely. I always trusted the Arab men in those days because I believed they were all religious, and so they would never do anyone any harm. He had all the tickets and I was never allowed to see them, so I assumed mine was a return and that he would make sure I got on the right plane back to England when my holiday was up. I didn't want to have to worry about any of these details. I was happy to let the men take care of everything.

Mum and Dad stayed with us until the plane took off. I was getting more and more nervous. 'If I don't like it there,' I asked Mum when the men weren't listening, 'can I come back?'

'Of course you can,' she reassured me. 'You can come back whenever you want.'

I felt very frightened as we went out to the jumbo jet waiting on the tarmac, to make my first flight ever. It seemed so big as we got close to it, and there was so much noise and wind. I looked back at the terminal building, hoping I might see Mum for one last wave, but the only people I could see were too distant to make out the faces. I felt a moment of panic, suddenly cut off from everything that was familiar, and on my way to something new and unknown with two men I hardly knew.

The three of us sat together in the middle of the plane. I was also sitting next to an English woman who was on her way to Abu Dhabi. Because I was nervous I just kept on chatting away to her as the plane prepared for take-off. She told me she was a midwife and she answered all my nosey questions very kindly and helped me to relax. Abdul Khada was on my other side and he slept for most of the ten-hour flight, lulled by the throbbing of the engines. I just kept fidgeting and talking and trying to distract myself.

We weren't flying straight to the Yemen, first we were flying to somewhere where we were going to have to change to a smaller plane. It was late afternoon by the time we landed and as we came out onto the steps of the jumbo the hot air hit me like a smothering blanket, knocking the breath out of me. I had never experienced anything like it before. To start with I thought it must be the heat from the plane's engines that I was feeling. As we walked across the tarmac I shouted to Abdul Khada over the engine noise, 'Where's the fan heater that's causing all this heat?'

He laughed. 'It is just the weather,' he explained. 'This is the normal temperature. This is not your cold, old England now.'

Although they had told us over the speakers where we were landing I hadn't been able to understand them very well.

'Where are we?' I asked.

'Syria,' Abdul Khada replied and I felt a sudden thud of fear in my stomach at being so far from home in such a strange sounding place. I panicked and for a moment I just wanted to run back onto the plane and go home to Sparkbrook and Mum and Nadia. I looked around me for some escape, but everyone was just walking calmly towards the terminal, unaware that anything was wrong. 'There is nothing wrong,' I told myself. 'You are just going on holiday.' The thought that Nadia would soon be joining me stopped me from doing anything and I kept walking with the rest of them.

They told us that our connecting flight was late arriving and we would have to wait in the airport lounge. I thought it would just be for a few minutes, but the minutes turned into hours. The heat was overpowering and there were crowds of people pouring in off different planes, jostling for space. They all seemed so familiar with everything that seemed so strange to me. I just drank Coke all the time and watched the passing parade of costumes and faces.

There were only wooden benches to sit on and I just felt so tired, hot and sweaty that I wished I had never started on the journey. I longed for a refreshing shower or bath. I decided to go into the Ladies to freshen up. I walked in and was hit by the smell. The room was full of people and the toilets were just holes in the ground. There was filth everywhere, I couldn't believe it. It was the first time I had ever seen such a sight. I ran back out as uncomfortable as when I went in, and told Abdul Khada what it was like, thinking that he would show me somewhere cleaner where tourists from places like England could go. He just laughed again and told me not to fuss. I sat back on the wooden bench and stared miserably around me.

Evening descended on the airport with a clear, star-studded sky, and the crowds in the lounge slowly began to thin out as more and more people went out to the illuminated planes on the runway outside, which seemed to glow in the dark. Eventually there were only about twenty people left behind in the huge, echoing terminal. They were all waiting for the same flight as us. We didn't talk much more and I became more and more depressed as the night became blacker outside. We had been there seven hours.

It was the middle of the night by the time our plane arrived and we were called out from the lounge. I was glad to see the back of the airport, but I was even more frightened of the idea of going in a small plane. It seemed so cramped and vulnerable inside compared to the jumbo.

This time I was seated by a window overlooking the wing, which seemed to me to flap in the wind as we took off. I was convinced it was broken and we were going to crash. I began to panic and told Abdul Khada what was happening. He explained that it was meant to move about like that. I believed him, but there was still no way I could have slept on that plane, however tired I was. We arrived at Sana'a airport at five in the morning, just as it began to grow light.

Sana'a is the main city for the Yemen and it is nearly nine thousand feet above the sea. It is sometimes called 'the roof of Arabia'. The air was so thin it made me feel light headed and short of breath as I walked across the tarmac. The sensations mixed with my tiredness and hunger to make me feel almost drunk.

This wasn't our final destination, we were going to have to go south to Taiz, a town closer to the village where Abdul Khada's family lived. Sana'a was a lot cooler than Damascus, partly because it was so early, but they told me it was the coolest city in the Yemen anyway.

The airport was in the desert outside the city, so there was nothing to look at as we came out through customs. I noticed that a lot of people were staring at the way I was dressed. I was wearing a knee length skirt, sleeveless cotton blouse, sandals and uncovered hair. There weren't many other women at the airport, but those that were there were wearing veils and long dresses in the traditional Arab style.

'What are they all staring at?' I asked grumpily.

'Don't worry,' Abdul Khada smiled kindly, 'not every woman dresses like that over here. In the cities there are a lot of modern women who dress more like you.'

Outside it wasn't a romantic desert of sand dunes like in the films, there just seemed to be a lot of derelict old stone houses and rough roads. We waited around for about ten minutes until a large white taxi arrived to take us on the four hour drive to Taiz. The three of us climbed into the back of the six-seater car.

I didn't take in much of the scenery as we drove, I was tired and hungry and still trying to recover from the journey. The two men talked to the driver in Arabic but I didn't take much notice of anything. It was all a bit like being in a dream.

When we reached Taiz I was disappointed by how small and dirty everything was. The roads were narrow and crowded. The houses and shops seemed to be almost touching one another across them. The heat made the smells of dirt and animals mingle with car fumes and the aromas of food. The car was slowed down by the crowds of people moving about their business in the streets, some with donkeys or even cows. There was a lot of noise and a lot of dust in the air. There was litter everywhere, discarded food and old fruit just lying on the street, crushed under the wheels of the cars and the feet of passers by. All the buildings were traditionally built, the same way they had been built for the last thousand years. From a distance it all looked very beautiful and exotic, close-to it was a mess of people, animals and taxis. There were some women wearing western clothes, but far more were wearing traditional Arab clothes, complete with veils covering their faces.

'I have a friend who lives here in the city,' Abdul Khada explained. 'We will go to his house. We will stay overnight, so you can have a good night's sleep, and then we'll travel to the village.'

'Okay.' I would have agreed to anything that meant we could stop travelling and have a wash.

We turned into a backstreet which was only a few inches wider than the car, and pushed through the people walking below the three and four storey buildings, looking for the right house. We finally stopped outside a big brown door.

'Come on, get out,' Abdul Khada said, 'we're here.'

The door of the house swung open as we climbed out of the taxi into the heat and dust and Abdul Khada's friend came out to greet us, wearing a full-length Arab skirt, which I discovered was called a *futa*. He was the same sort of age as Abdul Khada, but didn't speak any English.

We went in through the door to a massive, concrete hallway covered with patterned lino. Through in the living room there was carpet on the floor, and mats and cushions all around the room for us to sit on. These were all signs of wealth to a Yemeni, but I was used to English standards of living and thought nothing of them. There was a television, and an electric fan standing on the table

23

which was cooling the air. I felt sweaty, uncomfortable and tired after travelling for over twenty-four hours. My nerves seemed stretched like elastic. The owner of the house showed me the bathroom where I could take a shower and change. It was a big, western-style room, but still with a hole in the floor instead of a toilet. I didn't care any more, as long as I could wash.

Feeling better after a shower and wearing fresh clothing, I went back into the living room. The men were all sitting talking. As I came in they got up and told me they were going out to do some shopping so that we could eat. They left me on my own sitting on cushions in the corner of the room. I felt very lost and alone without Abdul Khada there to explain things and translate for me. As soon as the front door banged shut the owner's wife and two young daughters came into the room. I later learnt that the women are not allowed to come into the same room when the husband is entertaining other men, unless the men are relatives. As long as there are men in the house the women remain invisible, merely waiting out of sight for shouted orders to make food or drinks, or perhaps to usher the husband's young sons in for the visitors to admire.

This woman and her daughters didn't speak a word of English and I really wanted to communicate with them. I was beginning to feel very tired, hungry and far from home, and I just started crying. I couldn't stop myself, the tears and sobs just bubbled out. I felt I had been left on my own at the end of the world.

The woman came over and kissed me on the cheek. They all sat down beside me and tried to communicate. Their eyes looked so kind and full of pity for me. I felt I was being silly and pulled myself together. I gestured to one of the girls that I wanted a pen and a piece of paper. She went and got it for me and I started drawing pictures and writing words in English. I don't know why I was doing it, I just felt so lonely and desperate to talk to somebody. Everything I wrote down the girl copied. I still couldn't stop myself crying as I worked with them, and the woman started to cry with me.

When the men came back they wanted to know what was going on. 'Why are you crying?' one of them asked.

'I don't know,' I said. 'Ask her why she is crying.'

Abdul Khada talked to the woman in Arabic and told me she was crying because she felt sorry for me and because she wanted to communicate too. Years later I was to meet the woman again, when I was able to talk to her in her own language, and I discovered that she was crying that day because she knew what was going to happen to me, and couldn't warn me. I loved her for caring like that, but there was nothing she could have done by that time, it was too late for anyone to be able to stop what was happening, I was already in their trap with no hope of escape.

We had a little food, although I was too tired by now to be able to eat much, and that night they brought me a sheet and I lay down in the living room on one of the mats. I slept soundly at last.

CHAPTER FOUR

Taking to the Hills

The next morning I woke up early to the smell of eggs and onions cooking. I got up and washed myself and ate breakfast and then we said goodbye to the family. I was feeling much better after a good night's sleep. I felt that I was ready to start my holiday now, and I was looking forward to having some adventures.

'Can we go out into town and look round the shops?' I asked. 'I want to get some presents to take home.'

'There will be plenty of time for that later,' Abdul Khada told me. 'Today we are going to drive up into the hills of Mokbana to meet the rest of my family, and to stay at my house.' He warned me it would be a long, bumpy ride, so I packed some fruit and took some orange juice to keep myself going. Inside the house it was cool and peaceful. As soon as we came out of the great wooden door into the street, the noise and smells and heat hit us like a wall. While the heat was so oppressive I never felt much like eating, but I seemed to be thirsty all the time.

Abdul Khada suggested that I should write some postcards home, telling them I had arrived all right, and was having a good time. Then he would post them in the city and they would get to England more quickly. I agreed.

The only way of getting to the village of Mokbana was by jeeps, Land Rovers and Range Rovers. They acted as the buses and taxis for the whole area, because they were the only vehicles that could navigate the rough, winding roads up into the hills. Every street was full of ordinary taxis, but Abdul Khada had ordered a Range Rover for the day.

The sun was at its fiercest when we climbed into the Range Rover after lunch. It was driven by Abdul Khada's niece's husband. Abdul Khada seemed to know or be related to everyone we met. We weren't the only travellers, there were twelve passengers in all including Abdul Khada, Mohammed and me. There were two other women sitting in the front, completely veiled in black, and the rest of us were bumped and jostled together in the back.

We drove for an hour along a made-up road which was relatively smooth going. I was told it had been built by the Germans. The scenery on either side was nothing but dry scrubland. There were roadblocks and checkpoints every twenty miles or so, staffed by armed police and soldiers. They were mostly chewing *qat*, the local drug, and fingering the triggers of their rifles absent-mindedly. Each time they wanted to see our identity papers.

Everyone has to have a permit to travel in the Yemen, even the locals, but the soldiers didn't seem particularly interested in any of us. I found out later that most of these roadblocks were to define borders between tribal areas. In each of the villages everyone is related and belongs to the same 'tribe'. In the past there has been a lot of feuding and killing, and the army was supposed to be helping to keep the peace.

After an hour we turned off the main road onto a track which headed up into the hills. The other men in the Range Rover also seemed to be friends of Abdul Khada and his son. They talked and laughed as we drove. I guessed that most of the men from the villages must know each other. Bored by the scenery I began to plan what presents I would buy for Mum and the others at home. I ate some fruit and drank from the orange juice carton.

The villages we passed through were bleak and inhospitable looking, with few signs of life. Occasionally we would see a grubby child wandering aimlessly with a few sheep or a cow, as the skinny animals searched for something to eat on the stony ground, or foraging with chickens amongst the broken stones of old buildings. Groups of skinny, flea-bitten dogs wandered, scavenging amongst the buildings.

When we passed through the tiny villages we saw veiled women coming back from the wells with pots of water on their heads, and groups of older villagers standing around outside their houses gossiping. As the Range Rover approached they would all stop talking and turn to scrutinise the occupants. They seemed to stare especially hard at me; I guessed it was because I was still wearing western clothes and I wasn't veiled. We would stop in some of the villages to let people on and off. A few women, carrying water jugs on their heads, stopped to stare at us. Ragged, barefoot children stood with their fingers in their mouths. Little girls carrying water or brushwood on their heads like their mothers would avert their eyes shyly. The men of the villages, squatting on their haunches and chewing *qat*, waved and shouted to Abdul Khada, welcoming him back, I suppose, since he had been away for four years.

I could see they were talking about me, but I couldn't tell what they were saying. I just kept smiling and nodding as politely as possible and looked around me while they talked.

The flat-roofed houses looked hundreds of years old to me, little more than piles of stone in the desert, their tiny windows tightly shuttered against the blaze of the afternoon sun. They had been building houses the same way for a thousand years, so it was impossible to tell the new from the old. Each village was very isolated. Sometimes we would be driving for half an hour or more between villages without seeing any houses or any people.

One village we stopped at for a drink was called Risean. It had a little river running through it which had turned everything green for miles around. It was like arriving at an oasis. There were fields of crops and fruit trees all around. I stood watching the local people as they ploughed the fields and tended their village.

There were vegetables like potatoes, carrots, onions, lettuces and cabbages growing in the fields, and spice plants which I didn't recognise. There were even some vineyards, although wine is forbidden in the Yemen, but raisins are popular. There were fruit trees bearing almonds, walnuts, peaches, apricots, pears, lemons and things I didn't recognise but I was told were pomegranates.

Whereas there had been hardly any people to be seen in the other villages we had passed through, here everyone seemed to be out in the sun, working and busy. It was the most beautiful place and I hoped that I would be staying somewhere as lush and well cared for. All the people in Risean were black Arabs. I wanted to ask lots of questions about them but I didn't dare, so I kept quiet, and got back into the Range Rover when Abdul Khada said we were continuing with the journey. I found out later that the Yemen is close to black African countries like Ethiopia and Somalia, only separated by a short stretch of sea.

'You will love my village.' I realised Abdul Khada was talking in English to me as we drove on.

'Yeah?' I smiled back. I was looking forward to meeting some new people.

'We have wonderful apple trees and orange trees.'

'Sounds lovely.' I went back to watching the passing scenery, imagining that we were heading to another village like Risean, but the scenery soon returned to the parched, featureless desert which we had been travelling through before. I wondered when it would start to change back to green again.

As we went further up into the hills we began to get

wider views out over the countryside. The Range Rover changed down into bottom gear as it climbed the almost vertical rockface, bumping and grinding over loose boulders and rocks. After two hours of this we stopped in the middle of nowhere.

'This is where we get out,' Abdul Khada explained, and the three of us climbed down and stood by the side of the track. The men all shouted their goodbyes and the Range Rover sped off up the road in a cloud of dust. I looked around me, but I couldn't see any buildings. In fact I couldn't see anything except bare hills and a few scrubby trees.

'Where do you live?' I asked.

Abdul Khada pointed up the hill behind us. 'Up there.' He grinned, picked up my case and the three of us began to climb slowly up the almost vertical rocky pathways. I was beginning to wish I had never started on this journey. My sandals kept sliding from under me on the loose stones and I was feeling hot, dirty and thirsty again.

As we reached the crest of the hill the village of Hockail was spread out below us, and I heaved a sigh of relief. It certainly wasn't beautiful like Risean, but at least we had got there and I would be able to have a wash.

'Which is your house?' I asked, hoping it was one of the nearest ones.

'That one up there,' Abdul Khada was pointing away from the village to one house which stood out on its own at the top of the highest mountain around. Buzzards circled in the air beneath it. To get to it we were going to have to walk up a vertical precipice with rough steps cut in it. The sight of the house shocked me with its isolation. It towered, bare and desolate, at the top of this dry, empty, lifeless world. It looked big from down below, but it did not look welcoming or comfortable. Oh well, I thought, it's only for a night or two, then we will be off and travelling to visit Leilah and Ahmed. This awful-looking house just seemed like another part of the great adventure, and I was very interested to learn just how these people lived in their strange-looking homes.

The first house we came to belonged to Abdul Noor, Abdul Khada's brother. It was a tiny, single-storey building with a door and just two windows. I couldn't imagine how anyone could live in such a place. It stood directly below Abdul Khada's house on the cliff above, so that someone standing on the roof of the house below would be able to shout to the people above to tell them if there was something happening in the village, or if someone had come to visit them and was waiting at one of the other houses. The news from the road would get to Abdul Noor's house first, and they would shout it up to the house on the top of the mountain.

'Come on.' Abdul Khada led me to the bottom of the cliff.

'I can't climb that!' I protested.

'Of course you can,' he said, and led the way up the almost invisible pathway.

Miraculously a tiny goat track seemed to appear from the rockface as we picked our way up, with me desperately trying not to look at the sheer drop to the rocks below. Half way up I felt the loose stones crumbling under one of my feet, my sandals slipped around and I fell painfully on my knees, skidding down amongst the falling pebbles. I screamed and Abdul Khada grabbed my hand and pulled me back up onto the path. By the time we reached the top we had been climbing for about half an hour. I was soaked in sweat, my knees were grazed and bleeding, and every muscle was aching. The men seemed to be used to it.

Perched on the very top of the world, the house had barren, dramatic views out over hundreds of miles of hilly countryside in every direction. It was like a tiny island floating in the sky. The air seemed very fresh. By then it was coming close to dusk and the day was cooling down. The sun was disappearing behind the mountains

31

in the distance and all the animals had been taken into the house for the night.

As we arrived the family came out to greet us. There was Abdul Khada's wife Ward, his old mother Saeeda and his blind father. Then there was Mohammed's wife Bakela and their two little daughters Shiffa and Tamanay, who were about eight and five.

I was introduced to them all and I just kept smiling and nodding and wishing I could understand what they were saying. They all seemed to be very pleased to meet me, and very welcoming. I felt like I was an honoured guest for them.

All the women were wearing traditional Arab clothes, even the little girls, with the dresses to below their knees and then the trousers down to the ankles and flip-flops on their feet. Their heads were swathed in scarves to cover their hair, because girls have to show their modesty from the moment they can walk. When they are just around their own homes and villages the women are allowed to show their faces and their fringes, and their hair can hang out the back of the scarves in long plaits. As soon as they travel to another village or on a road where they might be seen by other men, they have to completely hide themselves behind veils. Everyone wore flip-flops except for the grandfather who had traditional shoes made of heavy wood with a leather thong nailed on.

Walking into the house was like entering a cave. I knew this was where the animals were because I could smell them behind the stable doors, and hear them moving around. It was so dark it took a few moments for my eyes to re-focus. Some chickens were running around our feet.

There were some stone steps leading up to the floor above where the family lived. All the walls and floors were stone, but had been lined by hand with a mixture of dried cow dung and sand, which gave the whole house the smell of a cowshed.

The stairs led first to a hall, which was bare except for a pile of small home-made cushions in one corner, and everyone's rooms led off this main living area. All the rooms were small and had stable doors wth big bolts on them. The doors were all very narrow, so that you had to turn sideways to get through them.

I found that I was indeed being treated like an honoured guest. Ward had given up her bedroom for me. It had some linoleum on the floor, which none of the others had, and it had five little barred windows, two in one wall and three in another. That meant that there was a breeze when the shutters were opened and I had views out over the hills in two directions. There was an oil lamp hanging from the ceiling which would be lit when the sun finally went down, and which gave off a smoky smell.

There was also a small black and white television, running off a car battery, which Abdul Khada had bought for me so I wouldn't get bored. I soon realised that I could only get Arab channels on it which I couldn't understand at all, and which didn't seem interesting. I didn't want to be stuck inside anyway, I wanted to be outside in the light and fresh air all the time.

The only furniture in the room was a single, metal bedstead with a thin mattress, a pillow and a blanket, and a raised platform along one wall, made of the same rough cow dung and sand mixture. This was where I would sit if I wasn't in bed. There was a similar one outside the front door, where the two old people would sit most of the day on a tiny mattress just soaking up the sun and looking at the views. Out there people respect the elderly. They are thought to have made their contribution to the family and they are not expected to undertake the chores; everyone else looks after them.

On the same floor was a room for the grandparents, another for Mohammed and his family, with the children sleeping on the floor, and a long, narrow room for Abdul Khada and Ward. Another stone staircase led up to the

33

roof, where we were to spend a lot of time, and on the way up there was a tiny, black kitchen with a wood-burning stove for cooking chapatis, which were their staple diet, and a little paraffin stove for boiling water or frying things quickly. Beside the kitchen was the bathroom.

I needed to go to the toilet and I asked Abdul Khada where it was. He took me to this tiny doorway in the wall and opened it. I had to crouch down to get in. Inside it was completely dark, except for a small circle of light coming through a hole in the floor in one corner. The ceiling was so low I had to stoop all the time I was in there, and stooping in the middle of the room I could touch all the four walls. I always had to use a torch to see what I was doing.

There was a bowl of water for washing, and to use the lavatory I had to squat over the hole. Everything that fell through the hole just lay on the rocks below the house, drying in the sun amongst thorn bushes. I was too embarrassed to use it while anyone was around, so I used to sneak in there at night. If I had to use it during the day I would go out on the roof first and look all round the house to make sure there was no-one around to see what I was doing.

There was one permanent container of water in the bathroom, which the women filled from the tanks below, for washing with after using the toilet. When I wanted to wash my face I had to get another bowlful of water and take in the little soap container which I had brought with me from England. There was no hot water, but the heat outside made you want nothing more than to be drenched with cold water all day long.

That evening I didn't question where the water in the tanks had to come from. It was there, just like in England, and that was all I cared about. In the following few days I learnt just how hard the women had to work to make sure it was there when needed.

That first evening I didn't feel hungry. It was all so

strange, I felt shy and I wanted time to catch my breath and work out what was happening. So I sat on the floor in my room with the door open and watched the family sitting down to their meal in the hallway outside.

They all sat on the cushions in a circle, lit by oil lamps, with a bowl of chapatis broken up and mixed with milk on the floor in the middle. They would then scoop the dough-like mixture out with their hands and eat it from their own bowls. They were all talking and laughing, I couldn't believe I would ever be able to bring myself to eat like that. I watched fascinated, unable to understand anything they were saying. Everyone drank water, although they bought some Vimto in because it was a special occasion with my arrival, and the return of the two men. Vimto is like a diluted cherryade, and they only bought it for celebrations.

I could tell that Abdul Khada was the centre of attention, having been away for so long. He did most of the talking, with everyone else listening respectfully. When they had finished eating the whole family came into my room to sit and talk. It felt good to be so accepted; I was looking forward to being able to tell my friends in England all about these people. Eventually they all went to bed, and I crept out to the bathroom to try to work out how to wash myself after the long, hot journey.

By the time I got to bed I felt very uncomfortable. The bed itself was hard to settle in. I didn't feel clean and I now felt hungry, but it was all still an adventure and I didn't expect to be staying in the strange house for much longer. I eventually fell asleep.

The next morning I was woken at dawn with the sounds of the cockerel downstairs and the women bringing water from the well and working in the kitchen. The mountains looked very dramatic from my windows, bathed in early morning light. Breakfast was chapatis again, but cooked in a frying pan with a bit of oil, and eggs. They also made a flask of tea for the family to drink during the day, black and sweet. They had bought some milk from the shop specially for me, knowing the English taste for milky tea.

For the next two days I lived as their unsuspecting guest. I was looking forward to getting moving and seeing some more of the country, and to meeting Leilah and Ahmed. Even though I had never met them, and I knew they didn't speak English, at least they were family, and that would give us a bond in this place so far from home. Although I was impatient I didn't say anything. I just waited for Abdul Khada to tell me what we would be doing. I played outside with the children most of the time. They tried to teach me some elementary Arabic words. They were very friendly, happy little girls and I fell for them straight away.

Abdul Khada was very kind to me for the next two days. He realised that I was worried about eating with my hands, sitting on the floor, and he brought me a plate and fork in my room and cooked me special food. On the second afternoon he walked down to the shops with me. To me they looked more like huts full of fruit, cigarettes, tins of food and other vital supplies. Although the women out there were not normally allowed to smoke, I was already a smoker and Abdul Khada knew that there was no hope of breaking my habit, so he bought cigarettes for me. All the time he was treating me like an English girl, as if I was his equal, not like the local women. I still had no reason to suspect that anything was wrong.

He was well known by everyone in the village and seemed to be related to most of them. Everyone stopped to talk to him and many of the older men, who had been to England to work in the past, came up to me to talk in English, asking me if I liked it in the Yemen. None of them gave me any clues as to the real reason I had been brought over.

When we got back from the shops Abdul Khada and I

36

were sitting outside on the platform, talking to the old couple and the children, when Mohammed's younger brother Abdullah arrived up the same path that we had first climbed. I knew there was another boy and I had been told that he was in another village about two hours' drive away called Campais. Abdul Khada owned a restaurant in Campais, which was next to the main road out to Sana'a. Abdullah had been helping his father to fix it up in preparation for opening. I had been shown pictures of the boy before I came out, but I hadn't taken much notice. I knew that he was fourteen, but he looked more like ten to me. He was a weak, sickly looking little boy, very thin and pale. The whole family came out of the house to greet him, and his mother took his bag in for him. Ward seemed particularly fond of her second son. Later I was to find out that he had been sickly ever since he was born and that made her specially protective towards him.

'This is my son, Abdullah.' Abdul Khada introduced us, we shook hands, very formally, just as I had with everyone else two days earlier. His handshake seemed weak, and his hand was smaller than mine. We all sat down again outside, and I went on talking to Abdul Khada and the others and took no more notice of Abdullah, apart from being polite. He didn't seem very interesting to me, but I wanted to get on with everyone in the family if possible, and get to know them. I wanted it to be a good holiday.

As the sun began to go down behind the mountains and the air cooled, we all went inside and sat in my room, still talking. After a while the rest of the family left the room. Abdul Khada sat on the blanket-covered platform, between me and the boy. I was in my favourite place next to the window, which was the coolest spot in the room. The boy was staring at the floor, saying nothing.

Abdul Khada spoke softly and casually to me. 'This is your husband.'

I thought it was a joke. I just looked at him, not sure whether to laugh or not. 'What?' I asked.

'Abdullah is your husband.' he repeated, and I tried to concentrate on the words he was saying, unable to believe that I was hearing them right. My heart was crashing so loudly inside my ribs that I couldn't be sure what I was hearing. I felt short of breath and panic-stricken.

'He can't be my husband.' I still couldn't tell if it was a joke or whether he was being serious. I couldn't understand what was happening.

Mohammed must have been listening outside because he came to the door and looked in.

'What's he talking about, Mohammed?' I asked.

'Abdullah is your husband, Zana,' Mohammed answered and I could see that they were serious now. I was trying to work out in my head what could have happened.

'How can he be my husband,' was all I could think to say. 'What's going on?'

'Your father arranged the marriage in England,' they explained, 'and your sister Nadia is the same. She is married to Gowad's son. We have marriage certificates, so it is real. You are married and Abdullah here is your husband.'

I sat in the breeze from the window, numbed, just shaking my head and saying over and over, 'It can't be. How could it have happened?'

My thoughts were going round and round in my head. Abdul Khada and his two sons went back to talking to one another in Arabic as if I wasn't there. Eventually they went out of the room and left me to cry. I guess they must have gone to have a meal. I didn't care. I just wanted to be back home with Mum. I wanted someone to turn to, someone to make it all come right. I had no idea how to handle the situation.

The room grew dark while I just sat there, staring into space, and then Abdullah came back to the room, and I

38

realised that it was night-time and he intended to sleep with me. Abdul Khada was with him.

'He's not sleeping in here,' I said. 'I want to be alone.'

'He's your husband.' Abdul Khada was firm. 'You must sleep with him.' He pushed the boy in and slammed the door. I heard the bolt being pushed across the door outside.

I didn't look at Abdullah, and he didn't say anything to me. I could sense him moving across the room. He didn't know what to do any more than I did. He climbed into the bed, and I lay down on the blanket on the platform under the windows. I wasn't going to get into bed with him. I didn't sleep that night, I couldn't stop my mind from racing over what had happened, looking at it from every angle, trying to understand what was going on in my life. I heard the wolves and the hyenas howling in the mountains, and the rustling of the animals underneath the floor. In the moonlight I could see the lizards on the ceiling. The hours ticked slowly by.

The next day Abdullah must have told his father that I hadn't slept in the bed. Abdul Khada was furious and began shouting at me. 'Why didn't you sleep with him?' he demanded.

'No way,' I said. 'I don't want to sleep with him.' I felt the panic rising inside me again every time anyone spoke to me. All day I was crying, following Abdul Khada around begging him to tell me what would happen to me, and to let me go home. He told me that I could not go home 'yet'. I grasped at this one ray of hope, believing that if I just hung on I could get through the nightmare and get back to my home in Birmingham.

'When,' I pleaded, 'when can I go home?' But he wouldn't answer me.

Abdullah seemed almost as scared as me. He must have known that someone was being brought over from England for him to marry, but the way I was and the way I dressed must have been a shock to him, different from the women he had known all his life. As far as he was concerned I was unclean and immodest. I guess he was frightened of me, but he was more frightened of his father.

They all ignored me, and left me to wander around the house in a daze. I went into Mohammed's room. Bakela had been ill recently and there were some tablets on the platform, I remembered seeing them before and I went in to look for them. I didn't know what they were for, but I thought if I could swallow enough of them they would be a way out of the nightmare. I went into the room and picked up the bottle. I went back into my room, emptied the tablets into the palm of my hand and swallowed them. Mohammed must have been watching me, because he ran into the room at that moment and got me by the throat, choking me and forcing the tablets back up again.

I liked Mohammed, I could communicate with him and I believed that he felt sorry for me and most of the time he was kind to me. 'Please help me,' I pleaded, but he just shrugged his shoulders.

'There is nothing I can do,' he said. 'No man can disobey his father.'

He was frightened of his father as well, even though he was a grown man with a family of his own. Arab men always obey their fathers, I discovered, even when they disagree with them. All I could think of doing was to continue refusing to co-operate until they got sick of me and sent me home. That night Abdul Khada came to me again and told me that I must sleep with Abdullah.

'I'm not going to,' I said.

'You are,' he said firmly, 'otherwise we will have to force you. We'll tie you down on the bed.' Mohammed came in and said the same thing. I could see by looking at their faces that they meant it. They hadn't expected to have any trouble like this from a woman, especially a young girl a long way from home. They were desperate to force me to do as they said. There was nothing I could do but submit if I didn't want to be forced.

40

They didn't need to lock us in together that night, there was nowhere I could run to. Abdullah came in and he did what his father had told him. I lay still and let him get on with it.

CHAPTER FIVE
Trapped

The next morning, when Abdullah and I got out of bed, I went to the bathroom with a torch to wash from the bucket of cold water. When I had finished I went back into the bedroom and found Abdullah's mother, Ward, making the bed and inspecting the bottom sheet.

'What's she doing in this room?' I asked Abdul Khada in the nastiest voice I could, although I knew what she was looking for. She was checking the sheet for blood to be sure I had been a virgin and that Abdullah had done the job properly. At that moment I wished I hadn't been a virgin, just so that they wouldn't have had the satisfaction of taking it away from me.

I hated them so much I could hardly control my tongue. I was as nasty to everyone as I could be, giving them dirty looks, scowling and being sarcastic to Abdul Khada and Mohammed, as they were the only ones who understood what I was saying. But they weren't bothered by anything I said or did. All the grown-ups just kept out of my way, and gave me funny looks every so often. I suppose they must have expected some sort of bad reaction initially.

After Ward left the room I went back in and sat down to think. All I remember of that day now was the two girls, Shiffa and Tamanay coming in and trying to communicate with me. They were really lovely children and I didn't want to offend them. They had no idea of what was going on, or of how I felt, but I just wanted to be on my own that day. All the time I was saying to myself, sooner or later Mum is going to find out about this, and she will get me out. Throughout the next eight years I told myself, every day, that I was going to get out of that village, that there was no way I was going to stay there for ever. It was that determination that kept me alive I think.

For the first few days Abdul Khada allowed me to stay in my room on my own. He brought me food and gave me a knife and fork so that I didn't have to eat with them. He used to cook English dishes like chicken and chips for me, but I really didn't want to eat anything. I wasn't hungry because I was so upset, and I was put off by all the flies. There is never a moment in the Yemen when there aren't swarms of flies around you and around any food which is left out. During the days it was the flies that plagued us, and during the nights it was the mosquitoes. I never got used to them. There was nothing you could do to stop the mosquitoes biting, but you had to try not to scratch the bites during the day. At first I couldn't stop myself and I scratched until I bled. I never stopped itching. It took an enormous strength of will to stop myself tearing open my own skin, but I learnt. Those first few days I couldn't face any food, I just drank Vimto and waited for something to happen.

My moods swung back and forth. One moment I was sure that it wouldn't be long before someone found out what had happened and came looking for me. The next I would remember just how long a journey it was from Birmingham and I could see no reason why Mum should ever be able to find me.

In moments of blackest despair I thought perhaps Mum had known what Dad was doing all the time, perhaps she had even gone along with it. If that was true then there was no-one else in the world I could trust except Nadia.

I wanted to see Nadia so badly, but the thought of my

43

little sister having to go through the same ordeal as me was unbearable. I had to find a way to stop her coming out with Gowad.

I had brought a book of notepaper and envelopes with me from England, so I started writing to Mum and Nadia. It was a very long letter, telling them everything that Abdul Khada and his family had done to me, begging Mum to help and warning Nadia not to come. I put it into an envelope and gave it to Abdul Khada who was going to Taiz. I told him it was just a note to tell Mum I had arrived and was all right. He didn't seem suspicious and said he would post it. I don't know if he ever did. Later he told me that he had but that Dad had got to the letterbox first on the day it arrived and had taken it, read it and hidden it from Mum and Nadia.

I did nothing for the next week or so, just sat outside the house, and went down to the shops with Abdul Khada once. Everyone still stared at me because of the way I was dressed, but I didn't care. I wanted to show that I was different, an English girl, not one of them. There were two ways down to the village. One was a main route, a bumpy road which started at Abdul Noor's house at the bottom of the cliff. This was where the cars went and where the men walked. The alternative was a back way down the side of a mountain and through the bushes where the women were supposed to go. At that stage Abdul Khada was willing to let me walk down the main way with him, but as I gradually became one of the local women I started having to use the back route like the others. They were wise enough not to try to force me to do too many things too quickly. They knew, I suppose, that they would be able to wear me down in the end.

In the village Abdul Khada bought me a lot of fruit, none of which was very good, but I was glad to have anything which I recognised from home. On the way back we stopped off at his brother's house. Abdul Noor was away working, leaving his wife and daughter-in-law

44

behind. The house was much smaller than Abdul Khada's because there weren't so many of them. It was all on one level, with rooms coming off one long corridor. We went in to meet his brother's wife Amina. She was a very kind and polite woman. Her daughter-in-law Haola was also living there. I was beginning to understand how normal it was for the women to be left behind in the villages while their men went off round the world to work.

I liked Amina and Haola a lot, they both seemed very warm and made me feel comfortable. Amina talked to me all the time and I really wanted to learn the language so that I could understand what she was saying. The house had a completely different atmosphere to Abdul Khada and Ward's. Amina was crying for me that day, but Abdul Khada told her off and said she should be strong. I could tell what he was saying from the gestures he was making with his hands.

After the first night, when he had told me they would hold me down so that Abdullah could rape me, Mohammed was nearly always nice to me, although he sometimes provoked me. He talked a lot and behaved as if nothing had happened. Abdullah, who was supposed to be my husband, stayed silent whenever I was around. He ignored me in the same way that I was ignoring him. At night we still had to share the room and I did everything I could to avoid getting in the bed with him. Every morning Abdul Khada would ask the boy what had happened during the night, and I think Abdullah told him the truth, that I wouldn't sleep with him, because Abdul Khada was always angry with me. One night when Abdullah tried to touch me I lost my temper and kicked him hard from one end of the room to the other. I know I hurt him because he told his Dad and I got told off again.

Even though I was fighting it all the time, I knew I would have to give in in the end, because I knew that Abdullah had to have sex with me. It was the law that a wife had to give in to her husband's sexual needs. Although I could make it as hard as possible for them, in the end they knew they could force me to do whatever they wanted.

Abdul Khada was determined that I should submit and he wasn't a man that you could disobey for ever, at least Abdullah certainly couldn't. He was a foul-tempered, bully of a man when he didn't get his own way. He expected to have absolute power within the family, and none of them had the courage to challenge his rule. In that society the men are always right and are free to do as they please.

I think they were hoping I would get pregnant quickly because they thought that having a child would make me settle down. They thought that once I had a baby to consider I would no longer want to leave the Yemen and go back to England. Abdul Khada often told me that once I was pregnant I would be allowed to go back to England to have the baby with Mum. He said the quicker I gave up fighting the quicker I would get back to Birmingham. They just wanted me to give in and accept my fate, and although I was determined never to give up fighting, I began to see the sense in letting them believe that I was coming round to their point of view. In my mind I could see that if I could fool them into trusting me I might get back to England sooner. But then I would find that when I next spoke to one of them I couldn't resist being sarcastic or unpleasant again. I hated them too deeply to be able to pretend otherwise most of the time.

One evening, about a week after they told me that I was married to Abdullah, a friend of Abdul Khada's came to call at the house. He came in to meet me and then went off to talk to Abdul Khada in his room. I was polite to the visitor and then I went into Bakela's room to talk to her. I was still wearing my English clothes, and I had my hair uncovered. A little later, when the man had gone, Abdul Khada came storming into the room.

46

He had a bundle of clothes which he threw at me and ordered me to put them on.

'What for?' I asked.

'Other men can't see you dressed like that,' he shouted. 'It brings shame on me to have a woman in my house appearing in front of men in those clothes.'

I looked at the clothes he had thrown at me. They were a horrible orange colour and covered in sequins; they belonged to Ward.

'I'm not wearing these,' I said, throwing them down. Abdul Khada leapt forward, his temper had finally exploded and he hit me across the face. I screamed, my head hurt and I was as angry with him as he was with me. I hurled the bundle of clothes back at him. He came forward with his hand up to hit me again. I leapt up at him and bit his thumb as hard as I could, not letting go, like a dog with a rabbit, biting and biting on his nail until I could taste his blood in my mouth. He was shouting in pain and the noise brought Mohammed running into the room.

'What are you doing?' he shouted at his father, and pulled us apart. The two men left the room, Abdul Khada nursing his bleeding hand, leaving me with Bakela, shaking with anger and fear. Ward came in once her husband had left and picked up the scattered clothes. I couldn't understand what she was saying, but with sign language she seemed to be telling me that I must put the clothes on now, or else Abdul Khada would go mad with anger. She seemed horrified that I had dared to make him so furious.

The two women kept coaxing me until eventually I agreed to try them on, over my own clothes. The material was heavy and shiny and itchy. I stood there in the clothes feeling so stupid and uncomfortable; Bakela squeezed my shoulder comfortingly and I could see tears of pity in her eyes. I took the clothes off again and shook my head. 'I'm sorry,' I said. 'I'm not wearing these.' I was determined not to give in to them, not yet anyway.

47

I went on being as nasty to everyone as I could, and Abdul Khada went on hitting me whenever I talked back to him, and took care not to give me a chance to attack him back. I don't think he knew what to do with a woman who just wouldn't do what he told her. He became more and more frustrated by my behaviour. I soon learned that everyone in the village was frightened of him and very few people liked him. All the kindness he had shown me at the beginning had been an act, covering up his meanness and now he was showing his real character.

The other women tried to involve me in the daily chores of the house, although they didn't force me to do anything at first. They tried to persuade me to take an interest in their work, and to volunteer to help them. I think they still felt sorry for me at that stage and they were willing to give me time to get used to the life before insisting that I worked for them. They used to cook the chapatis on the red hot sides of a stove, which had wood burning in the middle. Ward asked me if I'd like to help and showed me what to do. I looked inside and saw the flames licking up round the walls where the women were putting their hands. I felt the intense heat beating up onto my face as I leaned over the stove and I just ran away, I was so frightened. I could see that their hands were hardened to the burning, but mine weren't, to me it looked like a hideous sort of torture, like continually burning in hell, day after day.

There were two types of chapatis which we ate: fried and baked. The fried ones were made from flour which we bought from the shop, ready-ground. We would get in a few months' supply at a time, storing it downstairs in the house. The women had to carry the sacks up from the village on their heads and they nearly always seemed to burst. It was something I was going to have to learn, but at that stage it looked impossibly hard to me.

The flour would then be kneaded out into round pancakes. They would put some fat into a frying pan and lay the pastry into the hot fat until it browned on both sides.

Most of the time, however, they had to bake them by hand in the fire, which meant leaning into the stove and plastering the pastry onto the white hot sides of the oven. These baked chapatis were made with cornflower which the women would grind themselves with a big stone, an endless and back-breaking job which I would soon grow to hate. Once the sides of the oven were covered in these pancakes they would add more wood to the fire to build up the flames, and then watch until they saw the pastry puffing inside. After about five minutes they would pull them off the hot walls with their bare hands. When the time came I was going to have to learn how to flick them off quickly enough not to burn my fingers, but not so quickly that they fell into the flames. As they came out the chapatis themselves were burning hot and we had to get them onto trays as quickly as possible. When I started doing the work my hands blistered in the heat, but Ward made me keep going, and eventually the skin hardened and I became skilful enough to do it without burning myself. The chapatis were our staple food, either eaten whole, or flaked up with milk and butter and eaten with our fingers.

In the beginning, however, I refused to even try any of these jobs, and because I wasn't helping round the house I had nothing to do but sit and brood on what had happened to me. One morning, when Abdul Khada had gone down to the shops, I couldn't stand the sitting around any more. There was a track leading away from the house into the woods, where the women went to get water sometimes, I could see it from my room, it looked like a route out of the situation to me. I made up my mind in a flash, I was going to get away.

I was just going to run and run until I was out of the mountains and out of the Yemen. I had no idea how I was going to do it, how I was going to escape from the village men who knew how to hunt and track and fight in

49

the mountains, or how I would survive the heat of the days, I didn't know what I would eat or drink or where I would sleep away from the insects, snakes and wild animals. I only knew that I had to get away from the house and from Abdul Khada and his family, that anything would be better than remaining their prisoner.

There was no time to stop and think, I had to go while Abdul Khada was out. I ran downstairs to the back door. The old blind man was just going out and I pushed him out of the way, running out into the sunlight.

I ran as fast as I could down the hill into the valley with the stones skidding and flying under my feet, my legs pounding and my lungs feeling like they would burst. I passed the little local graveyard behind the house and kept on running. I didn't know where I was going. I could hear my own breathing in my head and I remembered Kunte Kinte, the slave in *Roots*, who tried to run away from the plantation where he had been taken. I remembered how they caught him and took him back for punishment, and I forced my legs to go faster.

The old man must have called for the others because Mohammed and Ward started chasing me. I could hear them behind me, and every time I glanced back they were closer, shouting at me. It was like a nightmare because my whole body ached so much from the strain of running, and I could see that they were going faster than I ever could. They caught up with me in the valley below. I had no idea where I was or which way to turn. There was nowhere to hide from them. Mohammed grabbed me and began shaking me violently. He was panting too.

'What are you doing?' he shouted. 'Where are you going? You are mad to try to run away like this. Come back to the house. My father will be back from the shops soon, and if he ever finds out that you have tried to run away he will be furious.'

I couldn't do anything but go back to the house with them. When we got there we found Abdul Khada waiting for us and I felt a wave of fear at what he would do to me. He was as furious as Mohammed had predicted, but there was nothing I could say to him. I had no explanation, I just wanted to get away.

The weekend before Nadia was due to arrive in the Yemen, Abdul Khada said he would take me down to meet my brother and sister, Ahmed and Leilah in Marais. I agreed immediately, thinking that I might be able to get them to help me. Abdul Khada had to take me because he had promised my Dad that he would. He told me I could stay with Leilah and Ahmed and their families for as long as I liked. I was confused by his promises, and already learning to distrust everything he said, but I felt it was a chance to escape. I packed my suitcase.

It was a seven hour drive from the village and, as always, we left early in the morning to avoid the hottest part of the day. We went in a Land Rover taxi which picked Abdul Khada and me up on the main road. We had packed some fruit to eat on the journey.

After driving for a while we began to come up into another range of mountains. The road was bumpy and badly made and started to wind sharply round hairpin bends. As we rounded a corner I looked out of the window and saw a sheer drop down below the wheels of the car. We were skidding and bumping along the edge of a cliff. I began to panic and screamed. I begged them to stop the car and let me out, but Abdul Khada told me not to worry and the driver kept going. The roads became worse and worse, and we seemed to get closer and closer to going over the edge with every bend. I was becoming hysterical with fear and the journey went on for hour after hour.

At one stage we drew in to a small lay-by and stopped for a rest. I climbed out to get some air. We were right beside a massive drop and I begged Abdul Khada to let me walk the rest of the way. He shook his head. 'Too far,' he said, and signalled me to get back into the car.

51

By the time we reached Marais I just felt like bursting into tears, I was so frightened and tired and hot. I climbed out of the car with my legs shaking, and the villagers all crowded round us, jabbering in Arabic and wanting to meet me. I kept asking Abdul Khada to translate for me, but there were too many people talking at once, all jostling forward, smiling and laughing.

Through the crowd I saw an old man hobbling towards us on a stick. He was a small man, his back arched with age. He had white hair and glasses.

'This is your grandfather,' Abdul Khada told me, and I burst out crying. I wanted to communicate with the old man and ask for his help, but I couldn't. Abdul Khada translated for us, so I couldn't tell him what was happening. I asked where my brother and sister were.

'Your brother is on his way,' they told me, and a few minutes later Ahmed arrived, running through the crowd. He was wearing traditional Arab dress, the *fota* with a shirt over it, but I recognised him immediately as one of the Muhsen family. He was crying even before he reached the car as he elbowed his way through the villagers. We clung onto each other, both crying, and climbed back into the car together. Abdul Khada still had to translate for us, because Ahmed hadn't spoken English since my father took him away from Birmingham when he was three. I was desperate to tell him why I was so frightened, but all I could do was ask polite questions about how he was and where my sister was. He said we could go and visit her now.

We drove off down some bumpy roads, through a valley to another village where they told me my sister was living. There was a lot of open land and fields full of corn all around the village. After the terrible mountain drive it all looked very flat and green, and well watered by the streams which we passed. We stopped at an old stone house and the people all came out to see us, smiling, polite and curious. They told us that Leilah wasn't there. She and her husband had gone out somewhere because

52

they hadn't known we were coming.

We drove back to Marais and Abdul Khada told me to say goodbye to Ahmed. 'We have to go,' he said.

'What do you mean?' I felt the tears rising again. 'You said I could stop here.'

'You can't,' he shrugged. 'Your sister Nadia is arriving from England tomorrow and you have to come with me to meet her.'

I wanted to see Nadia more than anything else so I didn't say any more. Abdul Khada told me to wait by the car while he went to buy something to drink on the journey back. He walked over to an open-air shop and started talking to the shop-keeper. A man dressed in a western suit and tie came up to me and started speaking in English. He was very aggressive.

'What are you doing here?' he demanded, looking me up and down. 'You've just come to upset Ahmed and Leilah haven't you?' I was surprised by his tone, but it was so good to hear someone else speaking English. I really wanted to ask him for help and tell him what was going on, but the words wouldn't come out and he walked off as Abdul Khada came back from the shop with some bottles of Coke. Abdul Khada could see I was upset and asked me what the matter was. I told him what the man had said.

'What man?' he demanded, looking around, but the man had disappeared. Abdul Khada seemed to be genuinely upset for me for a moment.

The driver climbed back into the Land Rover and Ahmed hugged me tightly. I shook my grandfather politely by the hand and, as we drove off in a cloud of dust, I looked back and saw Ahmed standing by the road waving and crying.

Later I was to find out more about the life which Ahmed had led as a child. Our grandfather was not quite the sweet old man he now seemed. Because he had hated his son, my Dad, he had taken it out on Ahmed. He had beaten him constantly as a child. Now that Ahmed was

53

grown-up Grandfather would not allow him to marry. This is one of the worst things that can happen to a man in the Yemen, since they are not allowed to touch unmarried girls and adulterers are stoned to death if they are caught.

Our grandmother had died before the children had arrived in the Yemen. Grandfather had gone off to Kuwait to work, leaving them with his new wife, our step-grandmother. Ahmed was a sickly child and the old woman had no patience with him. Both he and Leilah were left to cope as best they could for themselves in the strange, hot new land, not having any idea what had happened to their mother or father. They were fed on old, cold scraps of food and made to go barefoot and carry water on their heads from the time they arrived. They were sent out each night with no lights and told to collect wood. They often had to walk miles to find enough. They both came down with a severe illness, but there was no-one to care for them, they had to suffer alone. All they had to comfort them was their love for one another.

When he was thirteen Ahmed was taken by the army. The country was in desperate need of young men at the time as they were at war in several different areas, and because the life was known to be brutally hard no-one volunteered. Press gangs of police would swoop on the villages and carry off by force any eligible young boys that they found there, regardless of the pleas of their parents to spare them. When the press gang arrived in Marais they didn't want to take Ahmed, he looked too sick and weak, but the old woman called after them and told them she wanted him to go. Ahmed was terrified because of all the stories he had heard about army life, but they dragged him away, and he was still in the army when I met him. The life was just as rough as he had heard, but he grew used to it in the end, and would sometimes go back to the village with money and to visit his grandfather. It was just luck that he was there on the day we arrived.

I soon realised the Land Rover was heading back up into the mountains the same way we had come and I started to cry again. It was growing dark and I was so frightened that we would take a bend too fast and slide down to our deaths. I asked if there was another way we could go to avoid the cliffs and the loose rocks, but they told me no, and to stop complaining.

Crossing the same mountains in the dark was terrifying. Although I couldn't see the drops below us I knew they were there. I was practically hysterical by the time we reached a small, empty-looking town called Eb.

'We'll stay here for the night,' Abdul Khada told me, pointing to an old three-storey house. We walked over to it, with me carrying my little suitcase. An old man answered the door. He was letting out rooms to passing travellers to make some extra money. I got a bedroom to myself and I lay on the floor till the morning, shivering with tiredness, emotion and fear.

Men like Abdul Khada and Gowad, who travel all the time away from their families, have to hire agents to help them with their businesses and to take letters to the families and make sure the money they send home reaches the women.

Abdul Khada and Gowad's agent was called Nasser Saleh and lived in Taiz. It was his house where we were going to meet Nadia. We arrived there the next morning, expecting to see Nadia later in the day. It was a big, clean house and he was obviously a successful man. We went up a flight of concrete stairs to a big room which seemed to be full of men. I immediately saw Abdullah, my so-called husband, and then Gowad and his son and a bunch of men who must have been travelling with them. I suddenly saw Nadia sitting quietly in the midst of them all, looking as lost and tired as I must have looked two weeks earlier.

Her flight had come in earlier than anyone expected, and the moment I saw her I knew that my letter couldn't have got through. I was so pleased to see her, but at the same time I was so unhappy that they had managed to get her out of England as well. There was no chance of saving her from her immediate fate now, we were just going to have to fight together to get away. I was more worried for her than I was for myself because I knew I was better than her at looking after myself, and because she seemed so much younger than me.

'There's your sister,' Abdul Khada said. 'Go and explain to her that she is married.'

'I can't tell her,' I whispered back.

'Tell her,' he ordered me. 'It will be better if she hears it from you.'

'All right,' I agreed reluctantly, and went across to her.

Nadia stood up and we just looked at each other for a few moments. I could feel the tears welling up inside me, I felt as if my emotions were going to sweep me away and I was going to break down. I ran up to her and we hugged each other, I couldn't stop myself from crying.

'What's the matter?' she wanted to know.

I couldn't explain, everything had hit me at once: the horror of what Abdul Khada and his family had done to me, and what was going to happen to Nadia now, mixed up with the feelings from meeting my brother Ahmed for the first time the day before, and then the tiredness from the terrifying drive over the mountain roads. I wanted to pour everything out to Nadia, but I couldn't find the words and I didn't know where to start. She made me sit down and someone brought me a drink. I started to explain to her what was happening.

'You see that boy over there.' I pointed across the room to Gowad's son Mohammed. 'He's your husband.'

She looked at the boy and then back at me. 'What?' She couldn't understand what I was saying. The boy was only thirteen, even younger than her, although he was much stronger looking than Abdullah.

'Dad's married us off. He sold us for £1,300 each to Gowad and Abdul Khada.'

It was impossible to talk in the room with all the men and they wanted us out of the way. Abdul Khada showed

56

us to a small room and left us alone so that I could tell her the whole story from start to finish.

'Didn't you get my letter?' I wanted to know.

'What letter?' She shook her head. She seemed unable to believe that it was happening to her. As I talked I was aware that it sounded like some horrible Arabian Nights fairy tale, and yet it was actually happening to us.

'What are we going to do?' Nadia asked.

'We're just going to keep writing to Mum until one of the letters gets through,' I explained. 'It's the only thing we can do. Don't worry, we're together now and when Mum finds out what's happened she'll get on to the authorities and get us out. There's no way she will let them keep us when she finds out.'

'Perhaps Mum knew about it too,' Nadia suggested, echoing the thoughts which sometimes passed through my own head.

'I don't believe it,' I said vehemently, 'I'm sure she didn't know any more than us. I'm sure she believed their stories.'

'Yes,' Nadia nodded, 'I'm sure too.'

But neither of us could be sure. We just couldn't bear the thought that everyone had betrayed us, we had to believe there was someone out there who would rescue us. Without that we were left with no hope at all.

Eventually we went back to the big room where all the men were talking.

'Have you told her?' Abdul Khada asked. He looked at Nadia. 'Do you understand?' She didn't answer, her face had gone blank, from then on she was always quiet and unsmiling, as if she had been stunned into silence. She had changed in a few moments from the open, laughing, joking girl that I had grown up with to a sad-eyed zombie.

In the afternoon we were put back into a Land Rover and driven back to the villages. I didn't realise it at the time, but that would be the last time the two of us would travel in a car together for many years.

CHAPTER SIX

Living as Neighbours

The village where Gowad and his family lived was called Ashube. It was smaller than Hockail, but only a half hour walk across the rough tracks behind our house. Whereas in Hockail the houses are spread out over a wide area, Ashube is more tightly packed, with a friendlier atmosphere to it.

Driving from Taiz we reached Ashube first. The Land Rover stopped and they told Nadia to get out with Gowad and his son, Mohammed.

'Where's she going?' I asked.

'She's going to Gowad's house,' Abdul Khada told me. 'We'll come and visit her tomorrow morning.'

A sudden panic rushed over me at the thought of being parted from Nadia so soon after I had found her again. I started screaming and begging them to let us stay together. Nadia had climbed out and was crying quietly by the side of the road. I realised that I was upsetting her and quietened down. They shut the doors of the car and Nadia turned with the men to walk the few hundred yards from the road to the village. I couldn't watch her go, knowing what was going to happen to her that night. I just buried my head in my hands and wept. The car started up and we drove on to Hockail.

As we drove I was ranting at Abdul Khada, shouting that he was a maniac, that he would never get away with it, and that Nadia and I were going home. I called him

58

every name I could think of, in front of all the other people in the car. I knew it wouldn't do me any good, but it made me feel better.

The next morning I was the first in the house to get up. I got myself ready and then I followed Abdul Khada around like a small child, continually asking when we could go to see Nadia until he eventually agreed to take me down to Gowad's house. To get there we had to walk down the same path that I had tried to escape along a few days before. We followed the narrow path along past the fields with their low walls and hedges and through the dark woods, walking for about half an hour until we reached Ashube. The house was already full of people who had come to see the travellers who had returned from England. There were men in one room and women in another, as usual. Nadia was not with the other women. They showed me which was her room and I went running straight up there.

I found her sitting on the bed as I came in. We clung onto each other and started crying again. When she could talk she told me what had happened. Gowad had told the boy and her that they had to sleep together that night, but neither of them had wanted to. Mohammed wasn't as weak and sickly as Abdullah, who I was supposed to have married, but he was still only thirteen and was just as afraid of Gowad as Abdullah was of Abdul Khada.

'Gowad pulled me into the room,' she said, 'and locked the door. I sat down and waited to see what would happen. Then I heard him outside, shouting at Mohammed. I think Mohammed was refusing to sleep with me. I could hear Gowad starting to beat the boy really badly. Mohammed was screaming and screaming, it was terrible.'

She stopped for a few minutes to catch her breath, 'Then I heard the door being unlocked,' she continued, 'and Gowad flung him in to me and slammed the door after him, like throwing an animal into a cage. I will never forget last night.'

59

Later I asked Abdul Khada why Gowad had hit his son, and he explained that the boy had refused to sleep with Nadia because of the way she was dressed, and her immodesty because her hair was uncovered. He told his father that he hadn't asked for a foreign bride and he didn't want one, and that was when Gowad lost his temper and began hitting him. The only women that boys like Mohammed and Abdullah had met before us were their mothers and relations. Everything they had been told led them to believe that other types of women were bad, and then suddenly they were told that they were married to two of these terrible creatures.

Gowad's wife was called Salama, and she seemed to be more understanding of Nadia's situation than Ward was of mine. She seemed to feel very sorry for Nadia and used to hug and comfort her like a mother, but there was nothing she could do: she had to obey her husband like all of them, and she seemed to love and respect Gowad.

Although Nadia wasn't as violently nasty to her family as I was to mine, she still answered back and questioned Gowad on why he was doing this to her, but in a quieter way than me. Whenever she begged him to let her go back to Mum in England he would just laugh, but once he was out of the room Salama would come over and comfort her.

Gowad is a tall man. At that time he was quite fat, although he has lost a lot of weight since then and now looks skinny. He was bald and hard faced, a horrible looking man.

His house was similar to Abdul Khada's although it had fewer rooms because it was a smaller family, with just Gowad, Salama, their two sons and Nadia. The younger son, Shiab, was only five years old when Nadia arrived. Salama had another baby girl soon afterwards.

Nadia's room was similar to mine, with the same basic furniture. Although it was a little bigger than mine the windows were smaller, which made it seem stuffy and dark. The living room was a big, light, airy room and they did actually have a window in the bathroom so that you could see what you were doing during the day without a torch, and a ceiling high enough to stand up without hitting your head. They did all their cooking under a shelter on the roof, a traditional habit to keep the smoke out of the house. They, too, would boil kettles on little paraffin stoves and eat the same types of food.

To start with Gowad looked after Nadia just as Abdul Khada had looked after me, cooking her English food and buying her things he thought she wanted. They let us continue seeing each other for the first week that she was there. One day she would come up to our house with Gowad and his family, the next day we would go down to them. Each day we expected to hear from Mum, but no word came. We used to sit outside and watch the sky, dreaming of seeing a helicopter coming up over the mountains and swooping down to rescue us.

They allowed us to continue behaving like English girls for a while, and we used to go up onto the roofs of the houses and sunbathe. The tans we got then never faded while we were out there, even though we were soon to be covered in Arab clothes from head to foot and our skins would no longer be exposed directly to the rays of the sun. The heat is so intense out there that it must actually brown the skin through clothes. Of course the parts that were exposed, like our feet and hands, became almost black in the end, from working in the fields.

The only news I had had from England was on my sixteenth birthday, which happened a few days before Nadia arrived. They had all sent me cards out from England and a letter from Mum saying that everyone was all right and sending their love. It had nearly broken my heart to read the messages from all the people I cared for, who still thought I was having a wonderful holiday.

Mum later told me that she was really happy for me on the day of my birthday, imagining me dancing and singing with my new Yemeni friends and having the

61

greatest party of my life. At that stage she had had my postcard saying what a good time I was having. She said she felt proud that her daughters had been able to have such an opportunity to experience life in another country. If only she had known that we were by then helpless prisoners.

That was the last time I heard from Mum for a long time. They didn't allow any more letters to come through. I think the agent in Taiz would give the letters to Gowad and Abdul Khada, and they would keep them.

By now Abdul Khada was making me use the back route all the time to the shops or to Ashube. It was a scary walk, passing through dark woods full of snakes and scorpions. I knew there were wolves and hyenas out there, as well as the baboons which I often saw in the fields from my window. I was told that Abdul Khada was jealous of all the women in his family, and didn't like other men to see them. He was especially bad with me, perhaps because he knew that I wanted to escape and he couldn't trust me.

He was right in that respect. Whenever I came across men in the villages who could speak English I used to beg them to help me. They used to come to the house sometimes to visit Abdul Khada and I would try to get a moment with them on my own to plead for help, but they always ignored me. The men were all connected to Abdul Khada in some way, either by blood, marriage, business or a combination of the three. They intended that I should stay where I was, and not give any of the other local women any ideas about challenging the authority of their men.

It was hard to get to speak to them anyway because, whenever he had men visitors, Abdul Khada would tell me to go to my room and keep out of the way. At the beginning he let me talk to them just as I would have done in England, but he gradually became stricter with me as I became a local Arab woman in his eyes. The village men were scared of Abdul Khada as well, although some of them seemed to feel sorry for me. They all told me not to worry. 'Give it time,' they said, 'and you'll settle down and be happy. You'll forget your Mum and Dad now you're married.' I hoped someone would agree to take a letter to post for us in Taiz, but none of them would. I was too scared to actually hand a letter to any of them. I didn't trust them, I knew they would just give the letter back to Abdul Khada.

Abdul Khada decided that Mum needed to hear some news about how we were getting on. He told me that we were to make a tape which he would send. For a moment I thought this would give me a chance to let Mum know what was happening, but I should have guessed Abdul Khada was too clever for that. I had to make my part of the tape in a room full of men, and they told me exactly what to say. I had to talk about how wonderful the Yemen was, and how we were slaughtering a lamb for a celebration and how happy I was. I felt so depressed afterwards, thinking Mum would believe it all and not try to get us out.

Years later, Mum told me that Dad had hidden the tape from her, afraid that she would guess something was wrong from the tone of our voices. But he told all his friends that he had received it and my brother Mo smuggled it out of Dad's pocket so Mum could listen to it. As soon as she heard it, she said, she knew we were being forced to lie from the tone of our voices. We had tried to make our voices sound sad, despite the words we were having to say, hoping that Mum would guess.

When the men came back to the villages from abroad, they usually stayed for six months or a year, depending on how much money they had saved. None of them worked while they were in the Yemen, there was nothing for them to do. They just sat around talking and chewing *qat*.

Qat is a local drug which everyone uses all the time. It is grown in vast fields in the more fertile areas of the country, and looks like the sort of privet bushes which you see in front of houses in England. People buy it in all the villages, either from a stall or from a man who delivers it to the houses on a donkey, and they chew the leaves. It makes the farmers in the fertile areas very rich. The better quality *qat* comes from Africa and comes over to the Yemen daily on ships from Ethiopia. The locally grown *qat* tasted much more bitter and was not as good.

The men, and sometimes the women as well, tear off the leaves and chew them into a wad which they keep in their cheeks, spitting it out periodically, leaving lumps of green saliva everywhere. It seems to make everyone feel calmer and happier, putting them in a world of their own, and it helps to quell the appetite. In the Ramadan month they like to chew it in the evening because they say it keeps them awake, so that they can sleep during the day when they are fasting. They spend a lot of money on *qat* for special occasions like weddings and births.

I tried it for a while, but I didn't like the bitter taste and it made me sleepy rather than the reverse. For a while I used it like sleeping pills, but not for long.

Most of the men smoked cigarettes, but hardly any of the women were allowed to. The women are allowed to smoke from chalices, however, in which they burn a weed called *tutan*. It's like a block of wood which they buy in the shop. They burn some coal in the chalice, breaking the *tutan* up into bits, sprinkling it on top of the coal and letting it burn slowly. There is water bubbling away in the chalice as well, and they smoke it through a pipe. They use *tutan* a lot in Ramadan as well.

As the weeks went on Nadia and I began to pick up Arabic. Being surrounded by people speaking a language makes it easier to learn. Shiffa and Tamanay, the two little girls, would help me by pointing to things and telling me the words. It took me six months to be able to make myself understood and a year to be able to speak and understand it fluently. I also taught myself how to read and write as well. Nadia learnt it quicker than me, but then she was allowed to move around her village more freely and mix with other women, talking all the time with different people, whereas I was more isolated. For a lot of the time I was just stuck with Ward and she didn't talk to me much. Her silence didn't bother me because I hated her as much as all the others. I made sure my hatred of them came across. I just couldn't help my attitude towards them, and they all knew the reason why.

There was a regular pattern to the life of the land each year. The thorn trees which grew so densely on some parts of the land would be cut back once a year to make sharp and effective hedges along the tops of the stone walls to keep the animals in. If the men were home at the right time they would climb the trees to prune off the branches. If they weren't there, and they usually weren't, we had to do it. When they had dried out well, the spiky branches would then be bundled up and the women would carry them up to the house on their heads, and store them downstairs for burning on the kitchen stove. If we ran short of wood we had to buy it from neighbouring villages.

The snakes, many of them poisonous, would live in amongst the branches and twigs. They came in all shapes and sizes. I was frightened of the whole idea of them.

One day there was a big scream from the village and somebody came up to the house to tell Ward that her brother had been bitten by a snake. He had been travelling from Taiz to Hockail. He got out of the car along the way and was bitten on the toe. He fainted and they brought him back to the village. We all went down the hill to visit him in his house. There was a crowd of people there and he was stretched out on the bed, mumbling deliriously. There was no doctor to call in the area at the time, so the women were using an ointment which they made themselves. He was lucky, the ointment worked and he healed up a few days later, but

65

it made me even more wary of the snakes I saw basking in the sun in the afternoons.

The crops, like corn, bran and wheat, are all looked after by the women, from the planting of the seeds to the baking of the chapatis. It is back-breaking work which can sometimes be helped by the men hiring machines from one another to help their women. Abdul Khada and Ward would never hire machines to help us, they were well-known in the area for their meanness.

When a girl marries into a Yemeni family, she is expected to share the burden of the work with the other women in the family, relieving the older ones of some of the worst chores. It is one of the reasons why the men are so keen to buy healthy, strong girls for their sons to marry. Local girls are trained up for the work from the moment they are walking, taught how to carry water on their heads, to cook, clean and look after the land and animals. They are shown no other way and are taught to respect, or at least fear, their men.

Neither of the families we had been forced into were unrealistic enough to expect Nadia and me to take on the work from the first day. They were breaking us in gradually, curtailing our freedoms bit by bit, and building up our workloads. We were like animals who needed to have their spirits broken before they could be properly trained.

Gowad wanted Nadia to start wearing Arab dress, just like Abdul Khada did with me, but he wasn't as violent about trying to enforce his wishes. He seemed to prefer to take a patient approach. He knew Nadia wasn't going anywhere and that eventually he would wear her down and make her do whatever he wanted. Perhaps they could tell that Nadia was going to be easier to keep quiet and persuade to co-operate than me. But he did force Nadia to carry water immediately she arrived in the Yemen, whereas they let me settle in before they insisted that I started doing that.

To fetch water from the wells the women carry down

big, empty steel tubs, some of them slightly bigger than an average bucket, others much larger. It was an endless task, which often had to be performed a dozen times a day. Once they were experienced the women would carry the bigger tubs, holding up to ten gallons of water. At the wells there are cans which need to be lowered into the water on ropes, then pulled up and emptied into the tubs. Once the tubs were full I used to lift them onto my knees and then up onto my head, with a piece of cloth rolled into a circle and put on my head to protect it. Most of the other women don't need any sort of protection like the cloth, they don't even need to hold the tubs with their hands, they can walk quite normally and balance them without spilling a drop. They have plenty of practice since they start going to the well so young. Tamanay was only five, but she used to have to come down with us to carry water back in child-sized tubs.

When I started to learn I was very clumsy, always tripping over and spilling the water, making Ward very angry. 'She has to learn to do these things,' she would tell Abdul Khada, 'to give me a rest.'

We had the use of a well on a neighbour's land which we went to most of the time, and there was another about twenty minutes' walk away for the times when there was no rain and the first well dried up. There was concrete all around it, and gratings to let the water run into it. When we got there we had to take our shoes off to keep it clean. The first time I went down to the well near to Abdul Khada's house I was horrified to see all the frogs and insects hopping and crawling around on the top. We had to shoo them onto one side before we could get at the water. I dreaded to think what sort of diseases I would catch from drinking it, but when you are thirsty you have to drink whatever there is. The first time I drank it, it did make me feel sick, but I soon became used to it. It was natural rainwater and I grew to like the taste.

The first trip to the wells would be at about five in the

morning, when the women would get up to start breakfast and prepare the house for the day. If you went that early the sun hadn't come up and the water was still reasonably cool, if you left it too late the drinking water would be hot all day. During the day the tanks inside the house would often run dry and we would have to go down two or three times during the afternoon for more supplies. In the evening, as it got cooler, we would be back down there. Sometimes we would all do ten or twelve trips a day.

We often went in pairs, for company, and sometimes I would go with one of the children, or with Haola from the house below. On one trip with Haola we had to go to the far well. As we rounded a corner of the mountain we came face to face with what looked to me like a baby dinosaur. It was about four feet long and stood about two feet high. It was looking straight at us, its jagged jaws open and spitting.

'Let's go back,' I stammered.

'Don't worry,' Haola said doubtfully, 'they can't run as fast as we can. But don't go near it. If they bite you they don't let go, and they have to be torn off you.'

As we stood watching, the little dragon changed colour in front of us, and another local girl joined us on the path. She gave a scream, picked up a rock and began beating the animal to death. Its skin was so thick the rock just kept bouncing off and the creature writhed and spat and snapped at her. It took nearly fifteen minutes to die. As it died its tail curled up and the girl hooked it up with a stick. It hung there, and seemed to shrink as the air drained out of it.

'What are you going to do with it?' I asked.

'Take it home and cook it,' she said, laughing at the horrified look on my face. She dangled it in front of me for a few minutes, teasing me, and then threw it away over the rocks.

After I had been in the Yemen for a few years the rains stopped coming. It didn't rain for nearly two years, and by the last six months the water had dried up completely. People were walking miles from surrounding villages to find somewhere which still had some water left. There are wells all over the villages and once one has dried up people just have to go and take water from their neighbours – they aren't supposed to do it, but there is no other way to survive.

When we lowered the cans to the bottom of the well at the height of the drought, they came up with mud in them. We would drain the mud out and drink what we were left with.

There was also an old well at the bottom of the garden beside the graveyard, which no-one ever used for drinking water. The graveyard wasn't full of tombstones like in England. When someone was buried they would fill in the hole with cement and then write the name of the person in the cement before it dried. The well was like a little stone hut with a door in it. Because it wasn't drinking water we were allowed to wash our clothes there. If I only had a little bit of washing to do I would use the water from the tanks in the house, but Ward would tell me off for wasting clean drinking water that way. So I usually went down to wash them in a basin by the well. Because no-one used this well much it was always full and you could easily scoop the water out from the top.

The water in the wells would be hot by the middle of the day, and we would be able to use soap powder in it. We would then lay the clothes out on the rocks to dry, or take them back to the house to dry on the roof. More often than not I would do everything at the well, just to get away from the others in the house.

As we got to know each other better Ward and I liked each other less and less. We never really got on at all and I did everything I could to stay out of her way. I did get on with Bakela, Mohammed's wife, and I really liked her daughters. I often went down to the wells with one or other of the girls, and one day I was at the washing well with Shiffa, the eight year-old, when I decided I felt like having a swim.

'Keep a watch out,' I told Shiffa, 'I'm going to go into the water.' Although I couldn't speak Arabic then, I managed to make her understand and she agreed. I walked down the steps into the water in my clothes. It was cool and dark and I let myself slide right under the water. Looking up I could see Shiffa's panic-stricken face looking down at me. Although I could see her through the clear water, she couldn't see me and she thought I had drowned. I stayed under as long as I could in the cool, dark silence, not wanting to ever get out. Eventually my lungs forced me back to the surface. Shiffa made a great pantomime of being scared, and told me that she thought she could hear footsteps coming, so I climbed back up the steps.

We walked back up to the house and I was still dripping. Ward wanted to know what had happened and Shiffa told her. I was in trouble again because women weren't allowed to swim at all in the Yemen, and because they said there were poisonous snakes in the water.

From my window I would sometimes see the monkeys stealing corn from the fields behind the house. If the men heard that the monkeys were around they came after them with guns, to save the crops. During the dry seasons they became braver and more aggressive, and would come up to the wells to drink, running off when people came close.

Once, when I was on my way to the shops with Tamanay, we were passing through the fields at the back when I noticed that the monkeys were everywhere. I had heard about them attacking women and I was a bit scared, but Tamanay didn't seem to be worried, so we kept walking. When we got to the bottom of the hill she started to tease them with a children's rhyme: 'you, monkey monkey ...' Her antics made me laugh, but they angered the monkeys and one of them ran towards us with its teeth bared, sending us running up the hill screaming. It watched us go and then went back to eating the corn.

Some of them grew to be almost as big as gorillas, but most were about chimpanzee size. Once, on the way back from the well round the mountain, I came face to face with one of the big ones, sitting on a ledge eating a plant. He kept chewing and fixed me with a stare as I edged past on the mountain path, trying not to show him how scared I was.

The neighbours on the hill, who had the drinking well on their land, were a smaller family than Abdul Khada's. When I arrived, there was just the woman, who was a friend of Ward's, and her daughter. The father was away in England working and the boy, who was fourteen, had just gone to Saudi for his first job. I didn't get to see them much.

As I grew more able to communicate with the women I found out how resigned most of them were to their lives, and to being left behind most of the time while their husbands went off round the world. There was one girl in Hockail called Hend who came to visit me and told me that she was unhappy and wanted to escape to the city and live a modern life, but she already had six daughters and she was still in her early twenties. Abdul Khada found out she had been to the house and told me I wasn't to talk to her any more because she had a bad name in the village. She was very open and nice but I had to stop seeing her because she was indiscreet. I suppose girls like Hend and me were a threat to the men in the village, they didn't like the thought that we might stir up trouble for them amongst the other women, putting ideas into their heads and making them question the rules which the men laid down for them.

Everyone in the villages knows each other, and most of them are related through blood as well as marriage. The Koran encourages relatives to marry one another, and a lot of the women in Hockail were married off to

71

their cousins. Haola, Abdul Khada's niece, was one of the nicest women I met out there, and she had married her cousin. I didn't understand it, and I asked Abdul Khada why she would want to do that.

'We like that out here,' he explained. 'If Abdullah had had a female cousin of the right age he would have married her instead of you.'

I doubt if any girl would have willingly married Abdullah if they had met him. Abdul Khada would certainly have had to pay much more for a bride whose father knew what a bad husband the boy was likely to make.

None of the women in the village except for Nadia and me had actually been forced into marriage. If they hadn't wanted to marry the boys that were chosen for them they didn't have to. That was why it was so wrong that they had forced Nadia and me to do it, because it was against our will, and against their religion. In the Koran it says that a girl must be asked three times at the wedding ceremony if she wants to go ahead with the marriage. We didn't even have a ceremony. Most of the other women just went along with the choices that their families made for them, and made the best of it, although it was not uncommon for women to be granted divorces from their first husbands later on. Nadia and I didn't understand any of this at the time. We just had to take their word for it that we were legally married, although we couldn't see how it was possible.

Four weeks after Nadia arrived in the Yemen, Abdul Khada told me about the restaurant which he had bought in a village called Campais. He told me that he had to open it now to make some money, and he was going to be taking Ward and Abdullah with him to help. I was going to have to go with them.

I couldn't believe that he was asking me to leave Nadia again so soon. I just didn't want to be apart from her. I told him I wasn't going, I wanted to stay with my sister.

72

He said I had no choice, I must simply do as I was told. When I told Nadia what he was planning she begged Abdul Khada to let me stay, but he said it was impossible. He told us we could still visit one another, but we knew that if it was too far for us to walk, we would never get them to drive us. We were right: in the next six months we met up on only two occasions.

CHAPTER SEVEN
Alone Again

One of Abdul Khada's relatives arrived early the next morning with his Land Rover to take us all across to Campais. I felt so depressed as we set out, and the scenery did nothing to cheer me up, as it gradually grew more and more bleak and dry.

The village was beside the main road leading to the capital city Sana'a from the ports through which came most of the country's supplies. The majority of the buildings, including the restaurant where we were going to be living and working, seemed to be fairly newly built. The rooms behind the restaurant were certainly cleaner than Abdul Khada's house in Hockail. It was quite a nice, big restaurant, standing amongst a group of similar establishments on the main road. But I didn't care about any of it, I just wanted to be back with Nadia.

The town was a mixture of modern and traditional. Although there were big lorries going past on the road, carrying goods into the country, camels were still used to transport goods like sacks of corn around town.

The three ground-floor bedrooms in the house were larger than the ones at Hockail, with proper cemented walls, and there was indoor running water and electricity which we hadn't had in the village, where we had had to use paraffin lamps to see after six in the evening. We had to carry the lamps around with us everywhere we went, filling the house with their evil-smelling fumes. At least there was a shower in this house, although there still wasn't a proper toilet. Above the bedrooms you could go up onto the roof to sit. There was quite a large garden, surrounded by a high wall which we couldn't see over. Abdul Khada grew his own vegetables such as potatoes and tomatoes, and I used to like sitting there, away from the others. It took a lot of water to look after the plants in the heat.

It was much hotter than in Hockail and the red ants, flies and mosquitoes were everywhere. The only way to escape the ants was to sit on a chair with your feet up. Because of the heat and the insects I began to see the benefits of wearing traditional Arab clothes, with trousers to protect my legs from the bites. I began to cover my hair and wear long dresses over trousers. Outwardly I was being forced to become a Yemeni woman.

Ward and I worked all the time in the kitchen out the back, which was really just a hallway behind the restaurant, while Abdul Khada and Abdullah served the customers out the front. During the day the heat in the kitchen would become unbearable, even with the door to the garden open all the time. Ward and I hardly spoke, we were both growing to hate each other. One day she threw a frozen chicken across to me and ordered me to 'cut and cook it'. I shouted 'no', and threw it back at her.

Most of the time we just ignored each other, and I was left completely on my own with no-one to talk to. Because no-one would talk to me I concentrated on learning to read and write Arabic before I could speak it. Abdul Khada gave me the alphabet and I worked from there, reading children's books or whatever was around. It was pretty straightforward. Whenever I asked him for things like this he was willing to get them for me, which was unusual in that society.

None of the other women in the villages could read or write, the men wouldn't allow it. The women never received any education – the men made sure of that –

because if they had started to learn they might have begun to question the way they were made to live and argue with the men; that would have been unthinkable. The schools in the villages were for the boys only, and they had to attend from a very early age, just like in England. If the women from the villages were going to escape to the cities or to other countries, they had to rely on their men taking them, and not many men wanted to do that.

Each morning the routine in the restaurant was the same. Ward would boil up a huge kettle of water to make tea for the customers coming in for breakfast, while I cleaned up. Abdul Khada would cook up eggs and beans, with bread which was bought from somewhere else in the town. A boy used to come in to make the chapatis with a frying pan out in the front of the restaurant. People would pay the boy direct and he would hand the money over to Abdul Khada and be paid wages at the end of the week.

At lunchtime he would cook big meals with meat and potatoes and rice, and then in the evening another meal like breakfast, served from six o'clock until eleven. All through the evening men would come in to eat, drink tea and coffee, play cards and chat with Abdul Khada who would sit behind the counter waiting to serve them. We all had to help with the cooking out the back, including Abdullah, but in the evenings he would go out the front and talk to the other men, leaving Ward and me out of sight. Abdul Khada would be cooking things like the meat out the front while we spent most of our time boiling water, making rice and washing up out the back.

I would usually go to bed before they closed up at night, because there was nothing else to do. Life for the women in places like the Yemen is so boring. If you aren't working there is nothing to do but sit and think, for year after year. There is no stimulation or entertainment. The only company most of the time is other women who lead equally monotonous lives. All

76

there is to talk about is rumour and gossip. Stories spread through the Yemen like plagues, because everyone is so bored. They are so desperate for news about other people that they are easily infected with lies and misinformation.

From my bedroom window in Campais I looked out onto a brick wall, just like the walls which surrounded the garden and stopped us from seeing out, and stopped anyone else from seeing in. It was like being inside a prison. The men are able to go out for walks, drive their cars, or travel; the women are allowed to do nothing and go nowhere. The endless routine of the days nearly drives you mad. The only entertainment I had was my little tape recorder, with some tapes which I had brought from England with me.

I was lucky that Abdul Khada let me keep the tapes, because he was always saying that I shouldn't have anything to remind me of England. He believed that I would settle down more quickly into my new life if I cut out the old one completely. One day he came into my room and began searching through my bag.

'What are you doing?' I asked, but he didn't answer. 'What are you looking for?'

'These!' He pulled out the few photographs which I had brought with me of Mum and my family and friends. I used to get them out sometimes when I was on my own, to look at.

'They're mine,' I shouted, trying to grab them. 'Give them back!'

'No.' He lifted them up out of my reach. 'They will just make you unhappy. You shouldn't have any reminders of your old life. We are your family now.'

I tried to pull his arm down and get the pictures, but he held on to them and tore them up. Then he gave me the pieces. 'Throw them away,' he ordered, 'into the fire.'

'Please don't make me,' I begged.

'Throw them away.' He went to hit me and I ran out to

77

the kitchen and dropped the fragments of pictures into the fire as he told me. Every day I expected him to destroy my music in the same way, but he never did.

All through the day in Campais Ward and I would be cleaning up the house and washing up after the customers had finished eating. We weren't allowed to go into the restaurant when it was open and when the men were in there. Sometimes Abdul Khada would tell us what was happening when he came through to the back for something, perhaps that there were some American or German tourists out there, but most of the time we were trapped in our hot, steamy, ant-ridden, fly-blown world.

One day Abdul Khada asked me if I wanted to go to the beach for a day out. I could hardly believe it. I thought he was teasing me and I expected him to get angry and hit me when I said 'yes', but he didn't. He asked Ward if she wanted to come and she said 'no', but he insisted. We left early in the morning because the heat in Campais got up to 190 degrees in the middle of the day. We closed down the restaurant and he took Ward, Abdullah and me down to the Red Sea in a taxi.

It was only a twenty-minute drive to the coast. On the way there it was pure desert, nothing but sand, with telephone poles dotted along the sides of the road. Half way there the smooth surfaces of the foreign-built roads gave way to bumpy local tracks.

The coastal strip is known as the Tilhama, which means 'hot lands'. The land is completely flat for miles, like a tropical sandy plain which stretches away dramatically in every direction as you drive down from the mountains.

There were few signs of life anywhere. As we approached the sea we passed a few derelict stone houses which looked as if they had been half demolished. The deserted beach was just as beautiful as the ones which my Dad and his friends had described to

78

us before we came out to the Yemen, with perfect sandy beaches and palm trees – but this was to be the only time I would get to see them in all the years I spent in the villages.

It was as if nobody had ever been there before us, apart from a few old Arab fishermen out in their boats who looked as if they had been there since the beginning of time. They took no notice of us. We climbed out of the car, looking like a typical Arab family on a day out. The wind was whipping the fine sand up into our eyes.

'Do you want to swim?' Abdul Khada asked, smiling kindly.

I was scared to say 'yes' at first in case he was still just testing me, and when I said 'yes' he would hit me for immodesty. By then I was wearing a long Arab dress with trousers underneath and a scarf hiding my hair.

'Do you want to swim?' he repeated. 'You can go in in your clothes if you like. It doesn't matter, there's nobody around.'

I didn't need to be asked again. I took my sandals off and walked into the water until it was deep enough for me to swim, with my Arab clothes billowing out around me. The scarf came off my hair and floated behind me in the warm, salty water. I was a good swimmer in England. I had won my bronze and my gold medals at school; I used to love it. I squinted my eyes up against the sun as it reflected off the water, and stared out at the distant horizon. I felt like just swimming out to sea and not stopping until I reached Africa. Abdul Khada was paddling in the shallows, watching me.

'Don't go too far!' he shouted, as if he had read my mind, 'there are sharks.'

I had seen the film *Jaws* in England, and that was enough to make sure that I didn't go too far from the beach. I swam back to shore and walked up the sand. The heat had already built up and my clothes were dry within a few minutes. Lying on the sand, I felt something uncomfortable underneath me, and dug up some empty

79

lager cans. I guessed the men must come down to the beach at night to drink the alcohol which they are forbidden by law. The taxi driver had wandered off on his own and we sat on the sand for about half an hour, before we had to get back into the car and return to the restaurant. That was to be my only day at the beach.

One morning I woke up with a burning fever and a fearful pain in my chest. I tried to get up, but I was too dizzy and weak to stand and I collapsed back onto the bed. I told Abdul Khada how I felt, but he dismissed it. 'It's just the heat,' he said.

I wasn't able to get up that day and two days later I started being sick. Abdul Khada began to look worried. I felt so bad that I just lay down all the time. I wasn't strong enough to feed myself and I thought that perhaps I was going to die. I felt glad when I thought about dying, because that would be a way out of the Yemen. I didn't want to go on living by that stage.

Abdul Khada must have been frightened that I was going to die, because he said he would call a doctor. There aren't many doctors in the Yemen, but there was one in Campais, a Sudanese man who spoke English. He came to see me and told me I had malaria. He gave me an injection and some medicine.

For the next three days he came twice a day to give me injections. I gradually grew strong enough to stand and go back to work, cleaning and cooking in the kitchen, but I never felt really well again while we were in the heat of Campais, and the malaria returned to me twice. There was no doctor to help me again, I just had to fight it on my own. All the local women could do to help was make me drink camel's milk, which they believe is the cure for the disease. The milk is hard to get but tastes quite good.

Every couple of weeks Mohammed, Abdul Khada's son, would come over from Hockail to see his parents, and he would spend some time talking to me. It was great to have someone else there, even for a short time. I used to beg him to get me back to the village, so that I could be near to Nadia, but he would just shrug and tell me there was nothing he could do to influence his father.

One afternoon I was sitting out the back, as bored as usual, when I heard Abdul Khada shout 'Nadia', out in the restaurant. I didn't dare to think which Nadia it was he was talking to. Then there was a sound of running feet and he crashed through the doors from the restaurant, shouting for me to come because my sister was there. Nadia came through from the front and I saw her dressed in traditional Arab clothes for the first time. It was strange to see her like that, but it must have felt the same for her seeing me. I was so happy to see her.

We went to my room to talk and they left us on our own for nearly the whole day to exchange our news. Neither of us had received any letters from Mum. I told her that Abdul Khada had ripped up my photographs, and she told me she had some back at the village. We just kept on talking and crying. She told me how she was made to carry water all the time, and how Gowad had forced her hand into the fire to make chapatis and how badly she had burnt herself. She showed me the scars. She had a more sensitive skin than me and I could see that she had other marks from where she had scratched at mosquito bites. The scars would still be with her years later. She told me Gowad had hit her and kicked her in the ribs one day when she refused to sleep with his son, but Gowad's wife Salama had come to her rescue. I told her she had to keep her hopes up and stay strong because something would happen eventually to save us.

We both thought she had come to stay for a few days, but that evening Gowad took her back to the village. She begged him to let her stay with me for a little while, but he refused.

After they had gone Abdul Khada came in to talk to me. 'You see how happy your sister is,' he said.

'How do you know she's happy?' I snapped back. 'How

do you know how she feels?'

'I just know,' he shrugged. 'She's been getting on better in the village without you, she has settled down.'

'She's not happy,' I snarled. 'She hates you all as much as I do.'

They wanted to keep us apart because they believed I was a bad influence on Nadia, so that was the only time she was allowed to visit me while I was in Campais.

Some weeks later one of Ward's relatives came down to tell her that her friend in the house next door at Hockail had been struck by lightning and had died. Abdul Khada told me that we were going straight back for the burial. I put my veil on for the first time and got into the car with the others. I didn't care what they made me wear any more, as long as I got back to the village to see Nadia, if only for a few hours.

As we sped out of the town I realised that I was slowly becoming an Arab woman on the outside. Anyone looking into the car that night would just have seen a veiled woman, being taken from one place to another by the men of her family. No-one would stare any more at the strange English girl with her short skirts and uncovered hair. I had become truly invisible to the world outside the family.

We arrived late that night. Ward went straight up to the neighbour's house and I followed. As I approached I could hear a strange wailing noise coming from inside. I walked in after Ward, and the room was full of local women crying for their friend. The women would continue wailing until the hole was dug and the body had been buried by the men, with the wise man of the village making a speech and a prayer over the grave. The women were not allowed to attend the ceremony, just to watch from the house.

No-one took any notice of me, so I walked back to Abdul Khada's house and went up to the room where it had all started. I felt happy to be there after the long months in the restaurant. There was no mattress on the bed and Bakela brought me a blanket and pillow so that I could sleep on the deck under the windows. I was pleased to see Bakela and the children, Shiffa and Tamanay, and because my Arabic had improved while I was away I was able to communicate better. We sat talking for a while before I went to sleep, and I started crying again, telling Bakela that I wanted to come back to the village permanently. She didn't know what to say, she was crying too. They seemed like such friendly faces after my imprisonment with Ward in Campais.

The next morning Nadia heard that we had come back to the village for the neighbour's funeral, and she came running up to the house. We stayed together for the whole day in my old room, talking. Abdul Khada had said we would be staying that night, so when Nadia left to go back to Gowad's house that evening she promised to come back again the next morning. Ward was pleased that we were staying too; she didn't like Campais any more than I did, she just had to stay there because her husband told her to. She wanted to come back to be with her family, particularly her mother who lived down in the village and was now a frail, old woman. But women like Ward have a lot of respect for their husbands, whether they like them or not, and they never argue with their decisions.

That night Abdul Khada changed his mind and told us that we were going to leave for Campais immediately. I was horrified.

'But you said we could stay another night,' I pleaded.

'We have to get back to the restaurant,' he insisted.

'But you told Nadia she could come back and see me in the morning.' I was desperate at the thought of being torn away from my sister again.

'It doesn't matter,' he said, 'Bakela can tell her you have gone.'

I tried to argue with him, but he just became angry and I was frightened to push him too far in case I got a beating. So we had to pack up again and leave in the dark. I thought my heart was breaking as we drove off into the black, desert night, and I imagined Nadia climbing the mountain the next morning, expecting to find me in my room, only to be told that I had been whisked away again.

On one of Mohammed's visits to Campais, I overheard him talking to his parents about a marriage he had arranged for Shiffa to a boy in the villages. I could understand just enough Arabic by then to get the gist of what they were saying. Shiffa was only nine years old and it made me cry to think of her being subjected to the same fate as Nadia and me. Once Mohammed had gone Abdul Khada came out the back and I asked him what was happening to Shiffa. He told me that the marriage had all been arranged and that the boy belonged to a wealthy family who would look after her well. Apparently the boy's father had a good business in Saudi Arabia, and plenty of sons working for him.

I suppose it wasn't so bad because she was still amongst her people and could go back to visit her Mum most days, and she was still allowed to behave like a child most of the time. They didn't make her wear veils and behave like a grown woman for a few years. Bakela never gave any hints of how she felt about losing her first daughter so young, perhaps she just took it for granted that it had to happen. Shiffa's new family had a much nicer house than Abdul Khada's, right in the heart of the village, and it was a big family, so in some ways Shiffa was better off than she had been with us.

There is always money involved in a Yemeni marriage, with the boy's family paying the girl's family to 'buy' her. How much they pay depends on how wealthy the family is, how much the boy likes the girl and how much he is willing to pay. The fathers of the girls will have an idea of how much they want for their daughters as well, and they will haggle until they reach an agreement. Some of the girls are sold very cheap, some are very expensive. The husband is also expected to buy a certain amount of expensive gold jewellery and clothing for the girl. Abdul Khada used to buy me gold jewellery sometimes, but I never showed him any gratitude. He couldn't understand why that was, and I couldn't understand how he could expect it.

This sort of bartering goes on mainly in the villages amongst the more traditional families, but in the cities many of the boys will approach the girls' fathers and ask for their hands in marriage just like in Europe. The girls will get western-style weddings with gold rings and white dresses, although they get married in their houses not in a church or mosque. The bride and groom travel round the city in a posh car after the ceremony and, if they can afford it, they go on a honeymoon abroad. Things are changing slowly, but not in the villages. Even in the city, however, there would be no physical relationship before the wedding.

Abdul Khada told me that Mohammed had done a deal with the boy's father and that, although Shiffa would go and live with her husband's family, the boy would not touch her until she was fourteen. When I got back to Hockail a woman in the boy's family told me that he had broken his father's word and there had been blood on the sheet after the first night.

We didn't go to the wedding, even though Ward was Shiffa's grandmother, because Abdul Khada said he wouldn't shut the restaurant for another day. I think he was just being spiteful. Ward was very upset because she was fond of Shiffa, and I was sad to think that there would be one less person for me to talk to if I ever returned to Hockail. I really liked Shiffa.

I was told that it had to be a quiet wedding because it was so soon after the death of the woman next door. Usually they have great firework displays at their weddings, but little Shiffa was just shipped out to her husband's house in a car at night.

Her husband was a nice boy, and by the time Shiffa

was thirteen she had grown to love him. That year she became pregnant twice and lost both babies with miscarriages. A year later, when she was fourteen, she became pregnant again. By that time Bakela was living in the city and she took Shiffa there for the birth. At seven months she gave birth to twin girls in her mother's house; one baby died immediately and the other died a few days later.

Back in the heat of Campais it wasn't long before I became sick with malaria again. They didn't call the doctor this time, they just gave me the camel's milk. I guess Ward may have been asking to go back to the village as well, and Abdul Khada decided he had had enough of us. He must have decided then that he wanted to go abroad to work for a while, although he didn't say anything to us about it. So he sold the restaurant and we headed back to Hockail, six months after we had first left. I couldn't believe how easy it was to escape, when only a few weeks before it had seemed impossible. As long as Ward and I wanted to leave nothing happened; the moment Abdul Khada decided that he wanted to leave, we were able to go.

CHAPTER EIGHT
Back to Nadia

Two weeks after we got back to Hockail Abdul Khada announced that he was going down to Taiz on business, and that was the last we saw of him for months. About four days later I received a letter from him, telling me that he had gone to Saudi to his restaurant there. He said he hadn't told me that he was going because he thought I would be upset since I had no-one else to talk to in English. In a way I was upset because I didn't get on with Ward at all, but now that I was back in the village I had Nadia and that was what I wanted most.

I was also glad to think that I wouldn't have him bullying me all the time, although he was still able to control all our lives, even when he was in Saudi Arabia. His influence over Ward, Mohammed and the other men in the village, meant that he could always make any of us do what he wanted with threats of what he would do to us when he returned. I was slowly growing to fear him as much as everyone else, knowing how ruthlessly he would beat me if I displeased him, but I still remained determined to win in the end. We had to escape somehow. There had to be a way.

While he was away he would send money back to Ward through Nasser Saleh, the agent I had met in Taiz. Not everyone trusted the agents who handled this sort of business, the women often thought they had been cheated of some of their money along the way, but

Abdul Khada was too good a businessman for that, he always made sure he had a receipt and that nothing was lost. I think any agent who knew Abdul Khada's reputation for violence would have thought twice about cheating him.

Ward sometimes complained that she didn't have enough money to pay the bills which she was running up at the shops, but there always seemed to be enough to buy the necessities. If the bills got too high she would get someone like Mohammed to write a letter to Abdul Khada on her behalf, telling him that she needed more money, and it would arrive a few days later. The post always got through to Saudi very quickly, because so many people travelled back and forth across the border.

After a while Mohammed got a job in Taiz, in a butter factory, although he continued coming back to the family at weekends. He told me he loved the job and that they paid him good money, but it meant one less person for me to talk to around the house most of the time.

When we had got back to the village Bakela was pregnant. She seemed quite happy about it and she said she wanted a boy this time. I hadn't really thought about what would happen when her time came to give birth, I suppose I imagined that when the time came they would take her off to a hospital in Taiz to deliver her. I had no experience of childbirth apart from whatever we had been taught at school. Three months later I watched as Ward delivered her daughter-in-law's baby on the bare floor of her bedroom, with Bakela screaming in pain. I was horrified and frightened. What would happen if something went wrong? Would it be this painful for me if I got pregnant? Was everything going right? Should there be that much blood? I was relieved to think that Abdul Khada had said I could go back to England to have a baby if I got pregnant.

I had realised that Bakela was in labour a few hours before the baby was born. She was groaning and moaning, and went up to her room to lie on the floor as the contractions began to speed up. I went up to see if there was anything I could do to help, and Haola, Abdul Khada's niece, came up from the house at the bottom of the cliff. All the local women always came round to help one another when there was a birth, although not so many came to our house because we were a little way out of the village and word didn't spread quickly enough. Haola, Ward and the old woman were able to manage, and they didn't give me anything to do.

I just sat and watched and listened. I was shocked. They laid her on the floor, without even a mat underneath her, and with Haola supporting her head. There was no doctor or anyone medically trained in case anything went wrong. The women remained quiet and calm, running around, clearing up all the blood on the clothes. Afterwards we had to get lots of water and take everything up onto the roof to wash. When it was all over I realised that nothing had gone wrong, and Bakela had a healthy baby boy, but while it was happening I had no idea if she was meant to be screaming like that.

When the baby was out they cut the cord with a razor blade and Bakela climbed onto the bed. The other women made a small hammock for the baby with a length of cloth and some rope, tying it onto the ends of the bed so that it hung next to its mother. Mohammed was due back that night, and by the time he reached the house he had been told he had a son. He was overjoyed. Bakela was allowed to stay in bed for a week, having her food brought to her and having the baby washed by Ward. I took over her chores and helped with fetching the water with Shiffa and cooking the chapatis. I was moving a few more steps down the line to becoming a dutiful Arab wife and daughter, but in my heart I was still waiting for my chance to escape.

When a woman has a baby in the Yemen she receives a lot of visitors. Every day that week the women came in with presents and money. It is more of a celebration for a

89

boy, with more visitors and more money. It is very quiet if it's a girl. On the seventh day they circumcised him. The job is done by a particular man in the village. It is very expensive because they have to pay the man a fee, and they have to kill a sheep as well to cook for the family celebration. I suppose they wait a week to see if the baby is going to survive. The man who does the circumcising is not medically trained at all, but he inherits the job from his father.

To perform the circumcision he stretches out the foreskin between his finger and thumb and ties it tight with a piece of cotton. He cuts through the skin where the cotton is using a razor blade. Then he scrapes all round the edge of the penis until it's really clean. There is a lot of blood and a lot of screaming from the baby. Afterwards they put a bright red lotion like iodine onto the cut. The baby then goes back onto the mother's breast to quieten it down, and they put a pad between its legs for a couple of weeks so that it can't rub the wound and make it sore.

There is also a woman in the village who circumcises the baby girls. Salama had a girl while Nadia was there. Nadia watched the circumcision and described it to me afterwards. They hold the baby girl naked. The woman stretches out the two flaps of skin outside the vagina and drives a needle through them both. When the needle has threaded the two flaps together, they pull them out and cut them off with a razor blade. I wondered if being circumcised would lessen the pleasure that a woman can get from sex later on. I asked one woman and she told me that it didn't, that she still got pleasure from sex, but then I don't know how she could have imagined the alternative. I don't know why they do it, I suppose it is just tradition. Although they are happy to continue doing it in the villages, the modern women in the cities don't allow their baby girls to be circumcised any more. The men say it is unhygienic not to circumcise the girls, but the women who have any opinions on the subject don't agree.

The little girls in the village had been told that if they

didn't have those flaps of skin cut off, they would grow longer and longer as they grew older, and that scared them. They believe that, and they never learn the truth because they never usually meet women who haven't been circumcised. When they found out that Nadia hadn't been circumcised they used to crack jokes about it. One girl asked her what her flaps of skin were like, which upset Salama who thought it was very rude to talk about such things. Salama told Gowad about the girl who had made the joke and he told her off. That calmed the situation down, but it must have been something they frequently talked about behind our backs.

Every village has resident 'wise men'. These are also positions inherited through the families. The wise men are usually from families with more money than the others. They usually have big houses where other people can go to visit them and talk about their problems. They are given money for their advice. If a woman, for instance, is unhappy with her marriage, she has to go to a certain wise man in the village and tell him what she wants to happen and why she is unhappy. If that wise man thinks that the husband has done something wrong – like being unfaithful – he gets into contact with important people in the city and the woman might be granted a divorce.

A woman who divorces has to give up her children to the husband and go back to her own family to let them look after her. The husband would probably give the children to his female relatives to look after – his mother or his sisters. It is the fear of losing their children which is one of the main reasons why so many women out there continue to put up with their husbands for so long.

Once, when I went to the village shops, I met a local wise man who spoke a little English. He was a nice man and seemed the sort of person you could respect, but I was too shy to tell him my problems, and I don't believe he would have been able to help me. By then I knew how

91

fast gossip and news spread through the villages, and I knew that if I confided in someone what I was feeling it would soon be broadcast everywhere, and I believed at the time that I should keep it in the family. The only person I felt safe in confiding everything to was Haola from the house below ours. In spite of this everyone knew how I felt, and if the women asked me how I was getting on with my husband I would tell them I was unhappy and wanted to go back home, nothing more. I think they all felt sorry for me. The village women always liked to be nosey, and sometimes they would ask me how I coped with my husband being so puny and weak, and they joked about him. I never knew what to say to them, they just seemed pathetic to me when they talked like that.

When all the men are away working, the senior woman takes control of everything in the home. In our house that was Ward. She had the power to tell me what to do and I had to obey her if I didn't want a beating from Abdul Khada when he came back. Ward enjoyed using her power over me. Sometimes she would leave me without food for several days, or would just feed me cold scraps of food left over from the day before. Sometimes I would have nothing but tea and cigarettes for two or three days at a time. I would ask Bakela why I was having to eat cold food when they were eating hot, but she couldn't say anything because Ward was in charge. Ward was never as mean to Bakela as she was to me, but even when she was unkind Bakela would never say anything, she was always respectful to her mother-in-law. I could have made my own food, but Ward used to lock it up in her room, and only she had the key. Because we had our own chickens we had the luxury of fresh eggs, but Ward always gave them to the men or to Bakela's children, never to me. Nadia had some chickens as well and she would sometimes give me eggs and meat.

92

Later, when I had been in the village a few years, some of the other women confided that they knew how Ward treated me, and they told me that she had always been a nasty, mean woman. Even her mother agreed. All the other women seemed to be so kind and I couldn't understand why Ward was so horrible. The man in the house next door remarried after his first wife was killed. I used to go up and see his new wife and she would sneak food out to me.

One day, when I was chopping the wood for the fires, I glimpsed a small snake slithering away from me. I was terrified. I grabbed a piece of wood and hit it, killing it. I had heard rumours of people eating snakes, so I thought I would try. I chopped the head off, built a little fire with a bundle of sticks and put the snake on top and cooked it until the skin had gone black. I broke it open to eat the flesh. It didn't taste too bad.

Word got back to Abdul Khada in Saudi about how his wife was treating me. He wrote to me telling me that he had heard I was starving and having to go to other people's houses for food. I wrote back and told him that was true, and because he hadn't let me have any money of my own I had to rely on Ward, who was cruel to me. After that he wrote a letter to Ward and one of the village women had to come up to the house to read it to her. It told her to leave everything open for me. She was furious at being told what to do, but she was scared to say anything in case I told her husband again. She knew that I talked about her to other people, and she grew to hate me even more. She used to tell me that I would be stuck in the village for the rest of my life, living like the rest of them, that I would never go back to my 'lovely, luxury England'. I just ignored her.

After Abdul Khada left for Saudi, Abdullah started to get sick. He slowly seemed to grow weaker and paler. I became frightened, thinking that because I had slept with him I would probably catch whatever disease it was

93

he had. Mohammed was continually taking him back and forth to the doctor in Taiz to try to find out what was wrong with him. None of them seemed to know. Ward told me that he had always been a sickly child, always very skinny and not eating much, but he seemed to be getting much worse. They gave him medicine, but they advised him to go abroad to somewhere like England or Saudi for more specialist treament.

Mohammed started writing to his father telling him that Abdullah was ill and that he should do something about it. For a long time Abdul Khada ignored their pleas, until Abdullah was eventually too sick to even get up out of his bed. He was taken down to the hospital in Taiz and kept there for a few weeks, which I was really happy about. To be honest I just wished he would die, because then I would have been free to go back to England. It was nice to just have him out of the house for a few weeks, so that I could sleep on my own. Not that he had been strong enough to want sex for some time, but I still didn't want to have him around. I wanted my freedom more than anything else in the world.

Eventually Abdul Khada came back from Saudi on a visit, and when he saw Abdullah he realised how sick his son was, and started to make arrangements for him to go to England for treatment. He asked me if I wanted to go with him, but I didn't believe he meant it. I thought it was just a trick to see what I would say. He told me that he did mean it, that he had my passport and he would make all the arrangements if that was what I wanted.

I came to believe that he was telling me the truth. I had had to keep a certain amount of trust in him, because I had nothing else to cling on to. I had been giving him letters to send to Mum all the way through my time there, even though I became more and more certain he wasn't sending them because I never heard anything back.

This time he seemed to be sincere. I had been trying hard to get on with the family while he was away, even with Ward. He had been writing to me all the time he was away, promising that if I would just settle down with Abdullah I would be allowed to go back to England. He promised me that in every letter. I thought that perhaps now he finally believed that I had settled down and could be trusted to go back.

It took him a while, and a lot of money, to get a visa for Abdullah to leave the country, with the help of Nasser Saleh in Taiz and a letter from the doctor saying that Abdullah needed medical treatment urgently. I became convinced that he meant what he said this time and that I really was going to get out. I wrote a long letter to Mum telling her everything that had happened to us again, and asking her to help. I told her that Abdul Khada was letting me come to England with Abdullah, and that as soon as I got there we would have to do everything we could to help Nadia to escape. I asked Abdul Khada to post the letter for me, and he agreed. We continued to wait impatiently for the official papers to come through for Abdullah.

Then one day Abdul Khada came up to me in the house and said, 'You wrote a letter to your mother, which your father has sent back to me.' I immediately felt sure that he had never sent that letter, I was certain he had just opened it and was going to use it as an excuse to stop me going. 'Your father is angry,' he went on, 'and he says that you can't go to England with Abdullah.'

I had been so sure that I was going to escape this time that this was like a blow in the face. I started hitting and kicking him and crying. 'You're lying,' I screamed, 'you haven't been sending my letters, you've been opening them all the time.' I let all my pent-up anger flood out, completely uncontrolled. What I didn't realise at the time was that Mum had taken the children and left Dad, so all the letters I was addressing to her at the café were falling straight into his hands.

The arrangements finally came through for Abdullah

to travel, and they both left for England together, leaving me in the village again.

When Abdul Khada and Mohammed were at home together they often used to tease me about going back to England, saying, 'Shall we let her go then?' and trying to needle me. I think Abdul Khada enjoyed the power that he had to make me happy and unhappy. Although sometimes Mohammed acted like an older brother to me, listening to my problems, at other times he seemed to be jealous of me in some way. Sometimes he would ignore me completely, or talk about me to other people when I was in the room, laughing about me and my unhappiness. His moods swung back and forth all the time.

When the men were around we would always eat well, whereas the women would just eat chapatis when they were alone. Abdul Khada always wanted a cooked chicken or lamb in the evening, which we had to slaughter ourselves.

A large lamb would last for three or four days, so they would just hang the carcass by the kitchen door for the flies to swarm over, as they did over everything that was left out. Most of the local families would buy live chickens from people who bred them, but Abdul Khada's family bred their own. Whoever was around had to learn how to slaughter.

I learned to kill chickens with a knife, although some of the others would just pull their heads off with their bare hands. You have to have a bowl of boiling hot water ready to throw the body straight into. That kills the nerves instantly and stops it jerking around. After that you pluck it, open it up and clean out the insides, then wash it and cook it. Whenever I was killing a chicken I used to imagine it was Abdul Khada's neck I was cutting into.

One *Ead*, which is a religious celebration like Christmas in England, Ward said she wasn't going to slaughter the lamb, so someone else would have to do it. Abdul Khada's sister was up staying with us from the village for a few weeks and she said she would kill it. I went outside the house with her to help. She held the lamb down, standing on its feet and lifting its neck up so that she could slit its throat with a big kitchen knife. 'In the name of God,' she said in Arabic, as they always do before they slaughter something. As she pulled the knife across the throat she did it wrong and the lamb just kept struggling when it should have died immediately. I couldn't bear to watch. She was shocked by the way it struggled, spraying blood everywhere, and didn't know what to do.

'You're cruel!' I shouted. 'You've done it wrong.' I took the knife off her and cut the throat again as I had seen the men doing, the blood splashed out over my hands and arms, and the lamb died immediately.

I let her skin it, and she tossed the skin away for the wild animals which roamed the area. The locals told me that the hyenas which lived in the mountains were man-eaters, that they had been known to attack and bring down strong men who were out late at night on their own. Many of the villagers told stories of finding severed hands and feet left beside the pathways to the village after the hyenas and wolves had done their nocturnal hunting. They had once had tigers in the area as well, but they had become extinct with the felling of the forests.

I never saw any of the wild animals, but I heard them when I was in bed at night, howling in the distance and sometimes walking round outside the house, looking for delicacies like the lamb's skin which I had seen Abdul Khada's sister toss away. I could hear them below my windows, tearing at the skins and growling over them, snorting and snuffling up the food and squabbling amongst themselves.

All the men carried guns for hunting the local vermin and to protect themselves from the animals and bandits. One night I was lying awake in bed when I heard

97

shouting down on the road below the cliff. I went to the window and I could see torches flashing in the dark. The next day I was told they had been chasing a hyena which had come right into the village. They wanted to kill it. When the men do catch a hyena they kill it and take the teeth out as souvenirs.

Very occasionally we would get something different to eat. We used to eat tuna fish sometimes, with potatoes, and we always ate loads of rice with everything. The main drink was tea, which we made with tea-bags if the men were there, but the women would just use tea leaves when alone. The bags are considered a luxury item for the rich, whereas the leaves are for the poor. We also drank fresh coffee, bought off other families in the area who grew it.

When the men were away the women had to do everything. Once or twice a year we would plant the crops. Although some of the women would hire someone to bring oxen to plough the fields, Ward was too mean, and she made us do it by hand. Every day for a couple of weeks I would have to go out into the fields with a dagger, bending over to plant each seed individually. I had to keep working from early morning until late at night, right through the heat of the day, no matter how painful my back grew, or how blistered my feet and hands became. All I had to keep me going was drinking water. Bakela would help me sometimes, but because she had the children to look after Ward would send her back into the house, and take over some of the work herself. Ward was a strong woman, but she expected me to keep going all day long at the same pace as her. All the women over there are strong, even the very old ones are still working in the fields and houses, and carrying things around on their heads.

The crops, which were mostly corn for chapatis and wholemeal corn for the brown bread, would then take a few months to grow, depending on how much rain there was. Once it had grown and we had harvested it, we had to grind the corn. To start with we had to break it up by hand and bring it indoors in bucketloads. This caused my fingers to blister for four years before they finally hardened. The buckets we brought in would last for about a week, and we would have to grind the corn each day.

We would soak as much as we needed for the next day overnight in water. The next morning we would go downstairs amongst the animals and grind it, bit by bit, under a huge stone rolling pin. The continual strain made my wrists ache all the time. This was to prepare the corn for cooking and baking. It was the hardest job that the women had to do, and the only one that you would hear them complaining about. Later I found out that most of the other women in the village had machines to do it, which were like grinding wheels with handles which they turned. Other women would take the corn to the shop and pay the shopkeepers to grind it for them, so that all they had to do was knead it and bake it into chapatis. But Ward insisted that we did it ourselves in the traditional way, even though it meant us working all day long.

Some of the other women would challenge Ward about it, saying 'Why do you make the English girl do it the hard way?' But she would just say, 'Leave her, she has to learn.' So I went on doing it, every single morning, and if there were people coming to dinner it might take me three or four hours to do enough. If I was going to be doing some planting in the fields I would have to grind enough corn to last us a few days, so that I would be free to work outside. This was as well as fetching the water, collecting wood and cleaning the house with a small broom made out of a bundle of straw.

The house was always dusty from the air outside, and the lizards would come inside and lay their eggs in clusters on the ceilings. Cleaning was an endless process. No sooner had you done it than the dust would settle again and a new batch of eggs would appear. Sometimes

99

the baby dinosaur creatures would get into the house. One got right into Bakela's room when the baby was sleeping. I saw it first and screamed and Bakela ran in and beat it to death. Another time I found a snake curled up in a hammock with one of the babies.

We used to have a lot of tarantulas around the house as well. Sitting outside in the sun one afternoon, with my sleeves rolled up and my eyes closed, I felt something moving through the hairs on my forearm. Looking down I saw a big, hairy, black-and-brown-striped tarantula walking slowly over me. I watched, horrified, as my goose pimples rose around it. I hardly dared to breathe. Finally I couldn't stand it any longer and I flicked it off. It flew through the air and landed on the ground. I leapt on top of it, feeling it splatter under my flip-flop. I ran inside, crying hysterically, and told them what had happened. They shrugged. It was no big deal to them.

The scorpions were another source of danger. Walking downstairs in the dark one day, with an empty tub to take to the well, I felt a sharp pain in my big toe. I screamed and threw down the tub, sending it clanging and crashing down to the ground floor. Stumbling down into the light from the doorway, I found a giant, black scorpion hanging onto me with its pincers, swaying its body back and forth as it tried to get its tail over to sting me. Because of the angle it couldn't reach me. Bakela came running in answer to my screams, picked up a stick and banged it off, sending it hurtling across the room.

Nadia wasn't so lucky. The women out there grow plants called *mushkoor* in pots on the roofs of the houses. They have a sweet smell and we used them to scent our wardrobes and drawers, and to put in our hair. Nadia was planting new seeds in her *mushkoor* pots one day when a baby scorpion came out from the dirt in a hole she had dug and stung her hand. Salama heard her cries and came running up to see what had happened. She took her downstairs.

Once the poison was into her blood her whole body

100

swelled like a balloon, and her skin went red. I was terrified. I was sure she was going to die. The women used a local herb ointment, and after a few days of illness, Nadia recovered. Some people survived the scorpions' bites and some died, it was just luck.

We also had to work constantly with the animals. If they were inside they had to be mucked out, which I would do with my bare hands, and if they were going outside to graze we had to stay with them because of the wolves and hyenas. Staying out in the heat of the day was hard, so I would always try to find some shade to sit in, but it wasn't always possible. At least being outside meant I was on my own and free to think. I just remember always crying and hurting during those times.

The only time I had to spare by now was in the evenings, and then I used to go outside and sit with the old man, who spent all his days squatting in the fresh air. I used to talk to him about everything. He used to tell me about his past and how it was to live then, like how they had to break stone by hand to build the houses.

I used to tell him how unhappy I was, how badly I was being treated and how much I wanted to go home. He was very kind, but there was nothing he could do. He just tried to reassure me.

'Have faith,' he would say. 'Be patient, and you'll get back to England, don't worry so much.'

CHAPTER NINE

A Life of Pain

On one of his return visits to the village Abdul Khada decided that it was time to extend the house. Until then we had used the roof as a sort of terrace, now he wanted to enclose it and turn it into one large room, somewhere where he could take his men visitors when they came to the house. It took months of work to finish it, and Abdul Khada hired two men to do the actual building work.

We didn't have to get the stone in the traditional way, digging it out of the mountains like the old man had described to me. Now they built with big, modern breeze blocks, which arrived from the city in trucks, but we still had to carry all the bricks up the cliff path on our heads, two or three at a time. We also had to carry up the sacks of cement, which always seemed to split, with the powder coating us, getting in our eyes and mouths, and mixing in our sweat.

The trucks would leave the materials at the bottom of the cliff, and the men would be working in the house. I had to get the bricks and cement to them. Each time I climbed the path I had to take frequent breaks because the weight of the sacks pushed my head down and I was unable to take breaths. Every day for a week I climbed the path up and down, from early morning until late at night. Other people would come and help me sometimes, like Abdul Noor's sons, who were old enough by then to carry a bit, but I had to keep going all the time. Abdul Khada would sit outside the house with his Dad, watching and criticising as I kept coming and going.

I would try to speed the work up by carrying more on each trip, but it became too painful and Abdul Khada was angry with me for doing it wrong, so I just had to keep on going, with the piles at the bottom of the cliff never seeming to get any smaller.

Once all the materials were at the top of the hill, I had to help Abdul Khada to mix the cement on the lino on the roof. The problem was that we needed a lot of water; there was a shortage at the time, so we had to travel from well to well all over the village to find the odd bucketful of water to take back to the roof and pour into the cement powder. It takes an incredible amount of water to build a room.

It was impossible for me to get enough water to do the job on my own, so Abdul Khada had to get other girls from the village to help me, and again I had to keep going from early morning right up to the middle of the night, when I would go out with a torch. Sometimes Bakela would come out with me in the dark, because I was scared, but more often I had to go on my own. It was the only way to maintain the supply of water.

After two weeks of no rain there was a sudden downpour. It went on all day, and I cried with joy at the sight of it, thinking that now the wells would fill up and we wouldn't have to walk so far. The wells did fill up, but Abdul Khada knew it wouldn't last for long, and so we had to work doubly hard to get the water up to the house before other people took it, or before it soaked away into the ground. We kept three big tanks on the roof, and they had to be continuously filled.

Because there were other men working in the house we had to wear veils across our faces all the time, which made it even harder to cope with the intense heat as we worked. One of the three water tanks had been lent to us by Salama, Gowad's wife. When we discovered that she had one, Abdul Khada had asked me if I would go and collect it. I had immediately said 'yes', because I always took every excuse to go across to Ashube and see Nadia, even if only for a few minutes. I went with Tamanay, Bakela's youngest daughter.

'Don't be long,' Abdul Khada warned us, as we set out at about half past one, in the hottest part of the day. 'I want you back here by three o'clock.'

We walked across to Ashube, and the dust and heat of even that short journey had exhausted us before we got there. When we arrived at the house I asked Salama if we could borrow the tank and she agreed. I sat with Nadia for a few minutes and told her what was happening back at Hockail. I told her how hard I was having to work, and how Abdul Khada wouldn't let me rest.

'Let me come and help,' she said.

'No!' I almost shouted back at her. I never wanted her to have to suffer anything. I always wanted to take the pain on her behalf, as if she was still a kid and I was protecting her from the bad things in life.

We stayed talking longer than we should have, and I suddenly realised I would have to hurry if I didn't want a beating when I got back. We went back out into the blazing sun.

The water tank was enormous, almost as tall as I was when I stood beside it, but I managed to get it up onto my head with the help of Nadia and Salama. By then I was becoming quite experienced at carrying in the traditional way, and I set out back towards home as quickly as I could with Tamanay trotting along beside me, urging me on all the time. Along the way my flip-flop slipped on a stone, I stumbled and the tank crashed to the ground. I was beginning to panic because it was past three o'clock and I knew Abdul Khada would be furious with us.

'Look at the time, Tamanay,' I said. 'We've got to hurry, help me up.'

104

Poor little Tamanay struggled to get the tank back onto my head but she couldn't even lift it, she was only a skinny little child. The effort of straining to lift the tank, and the fear of what would happen to us if we were late was making her cry.

There was nothing for it but to lift the tank back up on my own. I started by crouching down and getting the tank up, and then I had to stand without it toppling off. Every muscle in my body seemed to scream with pain as I forced my legs and back to straighten. Distracted by the pain of my muscles, I didn't notice that a thorn from the hedge had lodged in my face, and as I strained to stand up under the weight of the tank the thorn bit in deeper and lifted the skin. The sudden pain in my cheek as the skin tore made me scream and I had to drop the tank back down again, making Tamanay jump back in fear.

I pulled the thorn out and the blood started to flow down my face, it seemed to be everywhere. I ignored the pain, more worried about what Abdul Khada was going to do if I kept him waiting any longer. Once again I crouched down, lifted the tank onto my head, managing to force my muscles to get me to my feet one more time, and we staggered on along the mountain paths.

We finally reached the house at about half past three and Ward helped me to get the tank off my head. She wanted to know why there was blood trickling down my face, but I couldn't find the breath to tell her. I thought I was going to collapse. She told me to go upstairs and tell Abdul Khada I was back. Each stair seemed like a mountain as I pulled myself up.

'Why are you so late?' Abdul Khada shouted as I came in, but I still couldn't find the strength to answer. Infuriated by my silence, he snatched up his leather shoe and hit me across the face with it, using all his strength. The shock of the blow sent me spinning backwards and I toppled down the stairs, unable to save myself. He came after me. 'Why are you so late?' he demanded again.

105

The words came tumbling out as I told him about dropping the tank, and the weight of it, and the thorn bush, but he wasn't listening. 'Go to the shop,' he ordered, 'and fetch some paraffin.'

Tamanay and I set out again to the shop, both crying all the way there. There was a man in the shop whom I had met before and who could speak English. I could see him looking at the dried blood and tears on my face, but he didn't say anything. The cut had stopped bleeding and the mark from the shoe was stinging, but was covered by my veil.

I lifted the three-gallon tank of paraffin onto my head but, as often happened, the lid was leaking, and it dripped slowly and steadily down onto my face, seeping into the cut and running over the bruise, soaking into my veil and nearly suffocating me with the fumes. I didn't care any more, I just wanted to die. I kept on walking in a trance.

By the time I reached the house my clothes were soaked through with paraffin. I thought Abdul Khada would hit me again. He stood looking at the state of me. 'Go and wash yourself,' was all he said.

Once I had washed and come back out again, he came up to me and kissed me on the forehead. 'I'm sorry Zana,' he said. I took no notice, it was too late for apologies by then. Bakela was crying for me, and anointed my cut with some ointment. They were all shocked by the way I was being treated, but nobody dared to say anything to Abdul Khada except his Mum, Saeeda. She used to tell him off for hitting me, but he took no notice of her. He would never answer her back – he was too respectful towards his parents for that – he would simply ignore her.

The old man wasn't able to see what was going on, but later that night I told him what his son had done to me that day. 'Just have faith,' he said. 'You'll go back home one day. Be strong.'

I soon discovered we weren't the only girls in the Mokbana area who had been taken from their homes in other

106

countries. Abdul Khada's family is spread out all over the Yemen. He has two very nice sisters who live in Rukab village, which was where Bakela originally came from. They had both married local men in the village and lived there with their children. It was about a half hour walk from Hockail. They used to come for visits quite often and I grew to know them quite well.

In village houses, rather than using paint on the walls, they use a sort of chalk stone which can be found in the mountain sides in certain places. The stone would be soaked overnight in the water until it became like a paste which could be spread over the walls. Rukab was somewhere where the chalk stone occurred naturally.

Ward was getting depressed with the house and wanted to brighten it up, so she sent Bakela and me down to Rukab to collect some of this chalk, so that we could redecorate. I was glad to get a day out of the house. She gave us some sacks to fill and we set off early in the morning.

Bakela was well known in the village but this was the first time I had been there. To get there we had to walk down a mountain side, and we could see the village lying at the bottom of the valley below. I was thirsty by the time we got there so we went to the house of one of Abdul Khada's sisters for a drink. As soon as we got upstairs the house began to crowd with people wanting to know who I was and to take a look at me. Although the women were all being very pleasant, I didn't like other people asking me questions at that time. I thought they were all too nosey and I used to give them a lot of sarcasm and back-chat.

Bakela was obviously very popular and some of the women offered to dig the chalk out of the cliff face for us and then all we would have to do was collect it up in the sacks. Bakela was very shy and tried to protest at their kindness, but they knew her well and dismissed her protests, telling us to have a rest and let them do the work.

107

They made us coffee and chapatis and we sat around enjoying our morning off. More and more women arrived to see us. I was just sitting watching them all chatting away when I noticed a young girl of about fourteen coming into the room. She was chubby, like a child, but very pretty and English looking with blonde hair which made her stand out from all the others.

'Who's she?' I asked Bakela.

'Another English girl,' Bakela answered. 'She came out when she was very young.'

I was eager to find out more. I walked out of the room, telling Bakela I was going for some fresh air, and asked the girl to come with me. We went downstairs, followed by a few others. I felt excited at meeting someone else in the same position as us. She had forgotten how to speak English but we were able to talk in Arabic.

She told me that when she was seven she was living in England with her parents, and with her sister who was nine. Her mother was English and her father was a Yemeni. Her mother died and their father remarried another English woman and brought them all out to his village, Rukab, for a visit. Her stepmother was unkind to the girls and wanted to be rid of them, and her father must have realised this was a good opportunity. Her parents disappeared leaving her and her sister behind with their uncle.

She told me that at ten her uncle married her to his son, and she described the way her mother in law treated her, which was just like the spiteful way Ward treated me. Her sister was married off to another cousin. She couldn't remember anything about England. She didn't know if she had any relations there, and the only English she could remember was counting from one to ten. She counted the numbers for me, very slowly, and I felt tears welling up at the thought of the life she must have had as a small child, which she now couldn't remember. When we left the village I wished her luck, but I knew she had no hope, because there was no-one left to help her.

The story made me cry, but during my time out in the Yemen I discovered that it wasn't uncommon, with girls being brought over from countries like America as well as Britain, and being left to lead peasant lives in the mountain villages. Most of them were never heard of again in their home countries, and I remained determined that that wasn't going to happen to Nadia and me. However long it took, I had to get back to my family.

Although he was so often cruel to me. Abdul Khada sometimes used to be very understanding of my problems. He used to bring me sanitary towels from the city, for instance, which none of the other women had. The others just had to use bits of cloth which they would sew inside their baggy trousers and leave throughout their periods. They tried to make me do the same but I found it too disgusting to even contemplate. I don't know how the other women put up with it, because in every other way they keep themselves scrupulously clean, washing every time they say their prayers, which means five or six times a day, and bathing themselves completely twice a day.

The whole family, except for the children, would say their prayers in their rooms, kneeling down on their praying mats and making all the correct movements. The women would talk quietly, but the men would make louder chanting noises. Each prayer session would last about ten minutes. To start with I didn't pray, but I would sit and watch them. As I came to understand the language better I used to listen to the preachers on the radio and I started to believe in the Muslim religion. I began to think that if I prayed, perhaps God would help me in my predicament. I would always pray in English, and every time I would say 'Please God, help me'.

It was hard to believe that any God was watching over the girls living in the Mokbana villages. Gowad's nephew used to live in a house above Nadia's on the mountain side. The nephew died in Saudi Arabia, and Nadia grew close to the widow who was left behind. She could have married again, but she chose to stay in her dead husband's house on her own and bring up his children, an eight-year-old girl and a baby boy.

She had to earn money to keep herself and the children, so she used to travel around the villages making clothes for the women. She taught Nadia how to sew, and Nadia got herself an old sewing machine and started making clothes as well. When she travelled to the other villages, the woman used to bring the boy down for Nadia and Salama to look after, and the girl would stay at the house doing chores while her mother was away.

I was at home in Hockail when I heard an outcry in the village below. Amina had heard some news from someone passing in the road and was shouting up to us. She told us that this little girl was dead and Nadia was involved.

I ran all the way to Ashube, having no idea what I would find. Nadia was very calm and collected when I found her and the little girl's funeral was already over. Nadia told me what had happened.

'We were looking after the boy,' she said, 'when a woman came down to the house and said that she had seen a child's flip-flops outside the well, and a tub floating on top of the water. By the time Salama and I got up there, there was already a crowd. They were all feeling around in the water with sticks, but none of them could swim. We squeezed through the crowd to the front and Salama told them I could swim. 'Shall I go in?' I asked, and Salama nodded. I was really scared of what I might find, but I thought perhaps there was still a chance she was alive.

'I dived in head first and swam around. The sticks had stirred up the mud and it was impossible to see anything, I had to work by feel. I got to the bottom and groped around, but I only stirred up more mud. I had to go back to the surface for air.

Nadia (left) and Zana, before leaving England for the Yemen.

Muthana Muhsen, the girls' father, November 1987.
(© The Observer and John Reardon)

In the Yemen: Nadia, Tina and Zana, December 1987.
(© The Observer and Ben Gibson)

Nadia, Tina and Zana, December 1987.
(© The Observer and Ben Gibson)

Nadia and Tina, December 1987. (© The Observer and Ben Gibson)

Nadia, Tina and Zana with Eileen MacDonald, December 1987.
(© The Observer and Ben Gibson)

Miriam (Mum) and Zana, at Gatwick Airport, April 1988.
(© The Observer and Ben Gibson)

Zana (left) and Lynette, after escaping from the Yemen.

Ashia (left), Tina (centre) and Zana. Shortly after escaping from the Yemen.

'I went down a second time and touched something soft. It was the girl. I pulled her to the surface and the men lifted her out. Her eyes were open and there was foam coming from her mouth.

Nadia, remembering her training from school, turned the girl over and tried to push the water out of her, but it was too late. She went on pumping frantically until the village wise man told her to stop. They took the body to the house and some of the villagers went out looking for the mother.

They found her coming back from her work and as soon as she saw them she knew something terrible had happened to her children. They wouldn't tell her what was wrong and she ran, crying, back to her house. By the time she got there she was beside herself with grief and they had to hold her up so that she could walk into the room where the body was laid out. Because she was a woman she was not allowed to stand by her daughter's grave at the funeral, that was the men's job.

To make a grave out there they dig a hole and then make another hole into the side of it. They put the body in the side hole and brick it up. Then they fill the first hole with sand and stand praying over it.

The widow woman had to watch from the distance, holding her baby boy.

CHAPTER TEN

An Ally at Last

After our arrival in the Yemen Gowad stayed in Ashube for two years exactly, before going abroad again. By then his son Mohammed, Nadia's supposed husband, was old enough to work as well, and he went to Saudi Arabia, like most of the men and boys from the villages.

Mohammed had grown physically from a boy into a man, whereas Abdullah, the boy who was supposed to be my husband, had not. Mohammed got himself a good job, working in a boutique selling perfumes and aftershaves. He started to send money back to Nadia and to his mother, Salama. He would stay in Saudi for six months at a time, returning each time for a few months' holiday.

The first time that he came back, Nadia became pregnant. Gowad was working in England by then and he wrote to Nadia telling her that she would be able to go there too, as soon as Mohammed had enough money saved for their tickets. It was the same story that Abdul Khada had told me. Once we became pregnant they felt that we would no longer want to escape or fight them, that we would settle down to being 'good' Arab wives.

Nadia had a straightforward pregnancy. She didn't suffer any morning sickness, or any of the other symptoms, except that her breasts started to grow. She didn't seem to be at all frightened at the prospect of giving birth in the village. In some ways she was very strong. In others she was easily led. I think that if it hadn't been for me she would have forgotten her English and become absolutely the sort of woman they wanted her to be. I went on at her all the time, telling her to keep resisting and to keep hoping. Without me there I think she would have allowed them to walk all over her.

Salama was quite good to Nadia during her pregnancy. She allowed her to rest, so that she didn't get too tired. She was allowed to come over to Hockail to see me right to the end. I used to go down to her as often as I could, to save her the walk, but Abdul Khada was in Saudi at the time and he wrote to tell me that I was to stop going down to Ashube so often. He didn't like the idea of Nadia and I spending too much time together. I suppose he imagined we were plotting our escape, and he didn't like the idea of me being out of the house unless it was to run errands. I suppose he also felt that if none of his spies could see where I was at any time, I was no longer under his control.

From then on I was only allowed to go down to see her once a week, for the day. The more used to the Arab life I became, the stricter Abdul Khada was about how I should behave. If I disobeyed him someone in the family or village would always write and tell him about it and he would let me know that he would punish me when he got back if I didn't obey him. Although I did as he said most of the time, deep inside me I never gave in, and I never stopped hating.

Salama never stopped Nadia from coming up to see me, but in the ninth month of the pregnancy I told her to stop because I was worried she was doing too much and it was a long, hot walk for her. So I was cut off from her by the time the baby was due.

Early one morning Nadia's next-door neighbour came up to our house, and told Ward that Nadia had had a baby boy in the night, and that everything was all right. When I heard that the birth was all over I was furious, I wanted to know why nobody had come to get me. They

113

said it was because it was so late at night none of the women would walk outside. If a man had come for me at night and word had got back to Abdul Khada, he would have killed me. It would have been unacceptable for a woman to be seen with a man in such a situation.

I ran out of the house, with Ward shouting after me, 'I hope you're going to be back by lunchtime.'

'I'm not coming back today,' I shouted back to her. 'I'm going to stay with my sister.'

I kept running all the way to Ashube, and into Nadia's room. It was full of women and the baby was asleep in the hammock beside the bed. I burst into tears, and I don't think I stopped crying the whole day. Nadia looked really well and calm. She told me to stop crying because I was starting her off. I was beginning to get ill again that day and I was slowly starting to lose my voice.

Nadia told me that she had started her labour quite late in the evening. It hadn't lasted long. Salama had run to the next village to get this nice old lady whom she knew, to come and help. Nadia told me there wasn't much pain and the woman had been very calm and soothing. The baby boy came about an hour later. It seemed incredible to me that my little sister had become a mother.

A woman was in the room with us and she was suggesting names. Nadia chose to call him Haney. Later we got a letter from Dad saying that he had heard about the birth, and telling Nadia what to call the baby. I don't remember what name he wanted now, but Nadia didn't take any notice. Haney was born on 29 February 1984, a leap year, so he only gets to have birthdays every four years. He grew up to become a beautiful child, looking exactly like his mother.

I stayed with Nadia for three days, sleeping in her room with her. I was feeling worse and worse and even by the first night I was feeling really ill and completely unable to speak. I had to whisper into her ear to communicate. The next day I couldn't get up off the

114

floor, and Nadia had to feed me with a spoon, at the same time as looking after her new baby.

She took to the role of motherhood straight away, with the same calmness and tranquility that she approached everything. She went on breast-feeding Haney for two years in the end. She obviously adored him and having him there made her more vulnerable and scared when I talked about going back to England.

'If we go home now,' she would say, 'they'll take Haney off me.' The idea terrified her. It made me worried to think that they might have found a way of stopping her coming with me when I found a way out.

When Nadia and I were together we used to cut ourselves off from the other women and be on our own together all the time. We talked a lot about the old days in England, and that was the only thing that made Nadia smile and laugh. There was nothing for us to laugh about in the Yemen. We schemed and planned and dreamed of ways to get away, each idea wilder than the last. We knew that our only real hope was to get a letter through to Mum in some way, to let her know that we were in trouble and to get her to look for help. We had no idea what she had been told about us, or what she believed was happening. If she had received the cards they had made us write at the beginning she might believe that we really were happy and enjoying the Yemen. We couldn't allow ourselves to think that, we had to believe that she knew we were prisoners and that she was trying to find us.

There was also the tape that Abdul Khada had forced me to make quite early on in our stay there. He had hit me and forced me to say that Dad was a good man and that we were much happier in the Yemen than we had been in England, and how lovely it was out there. It nearly broke my heart to make that tape, because I knew that it might put Mum off the trail.

Soon after Haney was born a qualified doctor arrived

in Hockail. He was a local man who had been abroad to train and obtain his qualifications, and then decided that he wanted to come back and practise medicine in his home village, to help his own people. He was a young man, and I used to visit him when I wasn't well, which was becoming more and more frequent. He didn't speak English, but I was able to speak Arabic well enough by then to tell him my problems. When I couldn't sleep he gave me sleeping pills. I started getting bad pains in my chest and he gave me some tablets which took the pain away. He seemed a very good doctor and a kind man.

His house was very different to the places we were growing used to living in. It was like a town house which had been moved to the village, complete with carpets, a refrigerator and a television. I suppose he must have had a generator to run all these things because there still wasn't any electricity in the area by then. It was the best house in the village and everyone used to talk about it. It had been built by his father who was one of the most important wise men of the village.

With each visit he became friendlier and I found that he was an easy person to talk to. I told him that I never got any letters from my Mum and I asked him if, when he was travelling back and forth to the city, which he did often, he would post a letter for me in a public post box. He was not keen at first, I suppose he didn't want to interfere in another man's family business. I had to ask him several times, but in the end he realised how important it was to me and he said yes, he would. He also agreed that Mum could write back to his post box number in Taiz, and he would get the letters to me in secret. That way we would be able to avoid Nasser Saleh and his censorship plans.

When I told Nadia that I thought I had finally found someone whom I believed we could trust, we both began to dream again of escaping. I still couldn't believe that it would work. I was terrified that someone in the village or in Taiz would open the letter and read it and report back

116

to Abdul Khada who would beat me for trying to betray him again. So I still couldn't put everything I wanted to say into it, I had to write to Mum in a sort of code, hoping that she would be able to read between the lines and know that I was calling for help. The letter was full of hints that I knew she would understand, but which would not alert anyone else.

I finally wrote the letter on a piece of paper torn from an old exercise book. I gave Mum the doctor's post box number. Two weeks later the doctor's wife came up to our house on a visit. When Ward went out of the room she whispered to me that her husband had a letter for me, and I should go down to pick it up.

The moment I had a chance I ran down into the village and arrived panting at the house. I couldn't believe it when I saw the envelope with Mum's writing on it after all those years. How could it suddenly be so easy to reach her when it had been so impossible for so long?

The doctor smiled at me kindly and asked if I would like to stay to read it. I thanked him, but said I wanted to be alone in secret somewhere. I didn't want to cry in front of him. I hid it under my cloak and went back to the house. My heart was racing in my ears as I scrambled back up to the house with my secret letter. I couldn't believe I was actually going to be able to read it, that someone wasn't going to spring out at me, grab the envelope and tear it to shreds, as Abdul Khada had done with my photographs.

I locked myself in my room and tore the envelope open. I felt sure that now Mum knew where we were we would be going home in no time. Now that I had received such a prompt reply to my letter there was no doubt in my mind that the other letters had failed to get through. I was crying so hard I had difficulty focusing on the words.

Although Mum had realised that something was wrong, she was obviously very confused because her letter was so long and so full of questions. She told me that she hadn't had any of my letters, although she had heard the tape which they had forced me to make.

Abdul Khada had sent the tape to my Dad, but Mum got to hear about it. When my brother Mo was visiting Dad one day he pinched the tape and took it back to Mum. She told me that she could tell I was being forced to say the things I was saying, but didn't know what to do about it. Dad was furious with Mo and told him he had to choose between him and his Mum. Mo chose Mum and didn't go to see Dad any more.

I was disappointed that she still didn't fully understand the situation, and that it was obviously going to take much longer to get out of the Yemen than I had been imagining while waiting to read the letter. But at least we knew for sure that she had had nothing to do with selling us as brides, and that once she knew about our plight she would be doing all she could to get us out.

Now that I had found a way of getting letters out I sent a stream of them, and received a stream back. Nadia and I became more confident about what we wrote and about letting people know that we were in contact with Mum, not bothering to hide what was happening from anyone. The doctor's wife would sometimes bring the letters up to the house quite openly and, although they didn't like it, the family didn't try to take them away from me. The doctor was a well educated man from a good family, he wasn't afraid of anything Abdul Khada could do to him. We had finally found an ally who was strong enough to help us.

Abdul Khada soon got to hear what had happened and he was too cunning to show his real feelings at this challenge to his authority. He wrote to me saying he was glad to hear I had received a letter from Mum and, pretending that nothing had happened, he acted like an old friend of the family and asked after her health. In fact there was nothing he could say since he had been pretending to send our letters to her for so long. I felt that for the first time we had managed to outwit him, but

118

our situation still hadn't changed. Even if Mum knew of our predicament there didn't seem to be anything she could do about it right away.

She told us in her letters that the first she heard of our situation was when some of my friends came into the café and told her that Nadia and I were married. They had heard it from a woman whose husband came from the Mokbana. Mum said that Dad had got our birth certificates out of her drawer while she was working in the shop. When she confronted him he told her that he had obtained legal marriage documents and that there had been two Yemeni men as witnesses.

Mum had gone mad at this, and screamed at him: 'How could you, they are my babies! They are mine. They are your daughters and you sold them.'

He smiled at her and said, 'Prove it.'

'I'm going to get them back,' she told him, but he just laughed in her face.

'You try it,' he said, 'there is nothing you can do. They are gone, like the other two.'

So Mum wrote to the Foreign Office, as she had done all those years before about Ahmed and Leilah, but they just wrote back to say we were dual nationals and the Yemeni government now considered us to be Yemeni citizens. They told her that the only way we could come home was if our 'husbands' gave us permission to leave the country, so that we could get exit visas.

Nadia's social worker, Mary Birchell, also started writing to people like the British Embassy and various charities, but they all came back with the same answers. They were sorry but there was nothing they could do.

She started writing letters to us at the post box number in Taiz which Gowad and Abdul Khada had given her, but of course she received no replies because the letters were all intercepted. Even if the British Embassy in Sana'a had wanted to help, they had no way of tracing us from the box number.

Lynette's Mum, Mrs Wellington, who was a good

friend to Mum, had also been helping her. She wrote a letter to the Queen asking for her help. A lady-in-waiting had written back very sympathetically saying that her letter had been passed on to the Foreign Office. Mum and Mary Birchell wrote to Nigel Cantwell, the chairman of a charity called Defence of Children International, based in Geneva. Mr Cantwell wrote back to say the same as the others, as Nadia and I were dual nationals because we were married, there was little anyone could do. But he had sought legal advice on one point regarding the marriages. Apparently, because Mum and Dad were never married, Mum was legally our sole guardian. Since her permission had not been sought on the marriages of her daughters, it was possible that the Yemeni Government might rule that our marriages were illegal.

I grabbed at this straw, feeling sure this would be our way out, because I was certain that the marriages couldn't be legal. How could they be? We had never been asked and we certainly hadn't agreed to them, and if our Mum knew nothing about them then they couldn't be valid. But Mum was very cautious in what she said to us, not wanting to get our hopes up. She didn't seem to believe that the Yemeni government was going to want to spend much time sorting out a couple of illegal marriages in a distant village. She was also frightened that Dad might try to take Ashia and Tina from her and do the same to them as he had done to us. Other people told me that Mum had a nervous breakdown during the years that we were out of touch, that all the pressures and fears and frustrations seemed to crush her spirit. But when she started getting our letters her fighting spirit returned.

What Mum *wasn't* doing was going to the press and getting publicity. I kept trying to tell her in my letters to do that and to let the public know what was happening. One or two of the old men in the village who came to visit the old blind man at the house would tell me not to worry, that I would get to go home. Most of them knew the British people, and if Mum told them what was happening, they would make sure the Government did something about it. I kept hinting to her in my letters to put it in the newspapers, but she didn't seem to understand, she kept trying to do everything herself. I still didn't feel brave enough to write completely openly in the letters, for fear of who else might read them.

Our correspondence was now regular, although sometimes there might be a gap of up to two months between letters, but that was nothing compared to the four years of silence we had already suffered. Mum started sending photos of the family to replace the ones that had been destroyed. Ashia had a daughter by then, about whom I had known nothing. Abdul Khada had a camera and he used to take pictures of Nadia and me, which I used to send back to Mum. I think he believed that gestures like that would make our claims of being held prisoner seem ridiculous. For months on end the letters kept coming and going, giving us hope that something was happening, and making us even more impatient to get out of the Yemen and back to our family.

CHAPTER ELEVEN

A Visit from Home

Abdul Khada went with Abdullah to England so that the boy could receive medical treatment, and while he was there he took him to meet Dad. I think Dad was shocked by how small and sick Abdullah was. All the others in their group of friends were laughing at Abdullah and asking Dad how he could have married his daughter off to someone like that. Dad was made to feel ashamed by his own friends, people who would never have criticised his actions if Abdullah had been like other men. Abdul Khada actually told me all this after he came back to Hockail on his way to Saudi, having left Abdullah in England to finish his treatment.

I never quite found out what the treatment was supposed to be, but Abdullah stayed in England for nine months but then had to leave because his visa had expired before they could cure him. The authorities knew that he had over-stayed the time permitted by the visa and this was entered on his record, only to surface again later and create one more complication in our lives.

Abdul Khada told me that while he was in England he rang my Mum and told her to meet him at Gowad's house, because Gowad was in Birmingham at the time. They met and Mum started asking him questions about me and Nadia and he told her that I was married and happy. He told me he had met my sisters.

Abdullah only came back to the village for a few weeks before Abdul Khada shipped him out to Saudi to join him there. He had grown a bit taller while in England, but he looked just as thin and sick as when he left. The treatment didn't seem to have done him any good. Abdullah's brother Mohammed contacted Abdul Khada and told him that Abdullah was in a bad way and that he should get treatment in Saudi. Abdul Khada agreed and Abdullah left the Yemen again. I was relieved every time he went, although I didn't take much notice of him when he was there.

A little while later I heard that he was undergoing a major operation. There was something wrong with one of the tubes leading from his heart. It was blocking the blood flow and had to be replaced with a plastic one. They said he would be under anaesthetic for 24 hours. Abdul Khada said that the boy only had a fifty-fifty chance of surviving. I prayed that he would die on the operating table so that I would be free to leave the country. When I heard a couple of days later that he had survived, I was disappointed. Abdul Khada sent a telegram to let Ward know that everything was all right because she was worried, and a few days later he came down to reassure her in person.

Abdullah stayed in Saudi for several months to recuperate and help his father in his restaurant. As soon as he was strong enough Abdul Khada sent him back to the village in the hope that now he would be able to make me pregnant. They had all been wondering why I hadn't got pregnant before, but I hadn't taken any notice of their talk. They thought it was due to Abdullah's illness and I suppose that may have been the reason. He looked a lot better when he arrived back after the operation, and he had started to put on weight at last.

I became pregnant immediately and in 1985 I missed a period for the first time since I had started having them. I knew immediately what it meant. I told Ward that I had missed and she was thrilled – they were all rejoicing. I didn't feel bad or ill, I just knew that I was pregnant.

123

I was pleased too, because Abdul Khada had always promised me that if I got pregnant I could go back to England to have it. I had been doing my best in the recent months to give him the impression that I was settling down at last and that I was getting on with the family. I was lying a lot by then, to make him feel confident enough to send me back to Birmingham with Abdullah to give birth.

Mohammed came back from Saudi at the same time as Abdullah, and Nadia became pregnant again at exactly the same time as me. Her son Haney was two by then.

Ward was not as kind to me as Salama was to Nadia during her pregnancies. All the way through I did exactly the same work as before. There were days when I didn't think I could manage, but I had to because Bakela had gone down to Taiz to join Mohammed by then and Ward refused to do any of the work herself, so there was no-one else to fetch the water, make the food, clean the house or look after the animals. Bakela had had another baby before leaving Hockail, but now she was out of the village, and I envied her that. She had escaped into the modern world at last, even if it was only to Taiz. Her baby was another boy, but he was sick when he was born, too small and sick to be circumcised. He had to be taken to Taiz for medical treatment. After that Mohammed decided that he wanted his wife to come to the city to live with him. So I was left with just Ward and the old couple for company.

Some days I was sure that I was nearly at the end of the nightmare, that if I could just convince them that I was a dutiful daughter-in-law, they would let me visit England, and then I would be able to escape. Other days I despaired of anything ever happening to change things. I went on doing all my chores, and Nadia would try to help me because Salama gave her time off. Other women used to come to the well when I was there and be shocked to see that I was still having to carry water when I was eight months gone. I became enormous, which is hard to cope

124

with in the intense heat.

In the last month I would try to grab as much rest as I could. One afternoon I was lying on my bed for a few minutes, when I heard Amina calling up from the roof of her house at the bottom of the cliff. She said a package had been delivered from Mohammed in Taiz and could we both come down and collect it. Ward went down first because it took me a while to struggle up off the bed and make my way down the rock-face.

When I got to the bottom I saw a small crowd of local people all whispering amongst themselves. I knew there was something going on because of the way they were looking at me as they talked. I looked down to the road but I couldn't see a Land Rover and I knew that it would still be there if it had just delivered a parcel.

Haola came over to me and spoke gently. 'Zana, your Mum is down on the road, waiting to see you.'

As I walked to the edge of the next cliff I saw a car drive off. I looked down and saw two people standing by the side of the road. There was a woman in a red shirt and a young man I didn't recognise. It was the first time I had seen a woman with her hair uncovered for some time. I stood and stared, and my heart seemed to turn over in my chest.

The tears were trickling down my cheeks and I could feel the emotions building up in my chest and throat as I slipped and stumbled down the path towards them. Mum stood by the side of the road with her arms outstretched just looking at me. As I reached her we both broke down and sobbed, and I fell into her arms. We hung onto each other for what seemed like hours. The village women gathered silently on the top of the cliff to stare.

When I finally let her go she gestured to the boy beside her. 'Say hello to your brother,' she said, and I realised that it was Mo. I would never have recognised him, he had changed so much in five years. Then he started to cry as well. I looked back to Mum and realised she was having trouble with the heat.

125

'Come on,' I said, 'I'll get you out of the sun.'

Even though I was eight months pregnant I started off up the path much too fast for her and she had to ask me to slow down. We reached Abdul Noor's house and we sat outside on the concrete deck in the shade. The whole village seemed to be standing there, just staring. I didn't know what to say.

Amina broke the silence. 'So there's your Mum, Zana, how do you feel?' I couldn't find an answer. I just started firing questions at her.

'What's happening? How did you get here? Have you come to take us back?'

'Let me rest and I'll explain,' was all she would say. 'Where's the house?' I pointed to the top of the hill and she couldn't believe her eyes. 'We have to go up there?' was all she could say.

Amina brought a cold drink out for her and she had a rest. I was anxious to get her up to the house and find out what was happening. I was desperate, I wanted to know everything at once.

It took us about half an hour to get Mum up the next hill, and when she got to the top she collapsed outside the house, not even having the strength to get inside.

If only I had known she was coming I could have got some extra food in, or done something to make the place more comfortable for her, but there was nothing in the house for someone from England to eat, just the corn which I was used to by then. Mum couldn't eat that. What seemed to terrify her the most were the flies which were swarming all over her, settling on every part of her skin. It was strange to see the place through new eyes again, and to remember how unfamiliar it had all seemed to me when I first arrived. It made me realise how I had gradually got used to things.

Haola brought up Mum's suitcase and volunteered to go to Ashube and get Nadia. I asked her not to scare Nadia because of her condition, just to tell her to come to see me and not to mention that Mum was there.

126

We went inside to my room and she began to tell me what had happened. Apparently she realised something had gone wrong almost as soon as we failed to return from our 'holiday' in the Yemen, although she couldn't tell exactly what. People coming over from the Yemen began to fill her in with news about us, and one or two of our letters began to filter through to her. When she realised just what Dad had done she left him and moved out of the café with Mo, Tina and Ashia. It was about a year after we had gone that she approached Mr Cantwell at the charity in Geneva and he started trying to help.

She said she was frightened to get publicity in case that upset the Yemenis and made them hide us even further away in the mountains. Mr Cantwell wrote endless letters to the Yemeni government, asking them to help, and only ever received one reply, saying that they would look into the case. Nothing else ever happened and Mr Cantwell told Mum that his research showed there were no maps of the area where we had been taken, and that there was obviously some bribery going on within the government and police forces of Taiz to make sure that no-one did anything about looking for us. Every attempt they made to find out information about us led to a dead end.

Then Mum was involved in a road accident. She was making a call in a public telephone box round the corner from her house in Birmingham when a car smashed into it. She was badly injured and had to undergo emergency surgery. She was offered damages of £6,500. She was told that she would get much more if she went to court, but she wanted the money urgently. Since no-one else seemed able to find us, she had decided to fly out to the Yemen and look for us herself, taking Mo with her. She told Mr Cantwell about her plan and he suggested that if that failed, then it would be time to talk to the press, since they had nothing much left to lose. She believed the accident was an act of fate, to bring her the money to visit us, and she wrote to tell us that she was coming as soon as the money arrived. She had to wait three years before she finally received the money.

On arriving in the Yemen she and Mo went to see the British Vice-Consul, Mr Colin Page. He was very rude and aggressive and told her that she was wasting her time, she didn't have a hope of getting us out and might just as well go straight back to England. He told her again that the only way we could leave was if we had the permission of our husbands. He wanted to know how she thought she would be able to find us. Mum told him the names of the villages, but he said he had never heard of them and that knowing the names would be no good anyway because there weren't any maps of the area.

As she was leaving the office, Mr Page told her she had better watch out for Mo, since 'they would probably want to get their hands on him as well'.

Realising that she wasn't going to get any help from the embassy, Mum caught a bus up to Taiz. I had told her about Nasser Saleh, Abdul Khada's agent, and suggested that if she came over she should talk to him. Mum already had a fuzzy picture of Mohammed from 1980, and she knew that he and Bakela were living with the kids in Taiz, now, where he had his job in the butter factory. For three days she trailed around the city, talking to anyone who could speak English and asking if they recognised either of the names or the picture, or if they had heard of the villages. No-one could help, until eventually someone recognised Nasser Saleh's name and took her to him. He sent for Mohammed to come to his house to talk to her.

Mohammed was shocked to see her, but was as helpful as he could be and agreed to arrange for them to be taken out to the Mokbana. He must have telephoned Abdul Khada in Saudi, because he called Mum to the phone and asked her to speak to him. Mum said Abdul Khada sounded angry and frightened. He wanted to know what she was doing there, and warned her not to cause trouble. She pretended that she didn't know what he was talking about, that she had just come out to visit her daughters. He said that he had a letter from Dad, authorising him to take us down to Marais in Aden and leave us there if she caused any problems.

She calmed him down and hung up the phone. Mohammed seemed to be embarrassed by what was happening and he confessed to Mum that Dad had sold us to Abdul Khada and Gowad for £1,300 each. It was the first time she had been told for certain.

She also told me that she had discovered early on that it was Nasser Saleh who had been intercepting our letters to her and hers to us. She had informed the Yemeni Government and Nasser Saleh had been put in jail for it. Abdul Khada and Gowad had had to pay to get him out. We had known nothing about this. When she found him in Taiz, he told everyone: 'This is the woman who got me into all that trouble.'

She and Mo stayed the night with Mohammed, Bakela and the children, and the next day Mohammed hired a taxi to take her to the village. As they drove out of the town, Mum and Mo were really shocked by what they saw, by the barren desert and the little stone and mud huts. It looked to them as if a bomb had dropped. Mum said it was like a nightmare for her.

After she had finished her story I started to tell mine, and I could see how shocked she was. There wasn't time to go into detail then, I just told her the main points. She had had no idea how bad things were. She hadn't realised that I had been hinting that she should go to the press. It all seemed so confusing for her.

When they told me that Nadia had arrived at the house from Ashube, I went out to meet her on my own, to prepare her for the shock of seeing Mum after all those years. She reacted just like me, throwing herself into Mum's arms and hugging her. Haney was two then, and he hung back, frightened by the sight of his strangely dressed grandmother.

Ward seemed to accept their arrival in the house with

129

no emotion at all. She didn't seem to have noticed anything special was happening, she just made drinks for the visitors.

When I had first seen Mum standing by the side of the road I had thought we were going to go home at last. As soon as I started talking to her I knew that there was no way we were going to be able to get away yet. I could tell that she hadn't done enough or got to the right people yet. I told her that she was going to have to go back to England and go to the press and start creating a stir, demanding that someone did something to help us.

We decided that she would need some proof of what was happening, and I suggested that I make a tape which she could send to Mr Cantwell in Geneva and which she could play to journalists. This time I would record my own words and tell the whole truth.

I still had my tape recorder, so I went up onto the roof on my own to talk into it, to make a plea to Mr Cantwell to help us. It was very hard to talk into the microphone. I didn't know where to begin, and I had trouble thinking of the right words in English. I kept bursting into tears as I talked, so I would have to switch off, staring out at the mountains until I was calm enough to go on. It took me hours, but eventually I managed to fill the tape and took it down to Mum. I told her not to listen to it, because I knew the things I had said on it about being hit by Abdul Khada would have upset her. I told her to just pack it in her bag to take it with her.

She stayed with us for two weeks, some of the time with me and some with Nadia. I knew she would get upset if she saw how hard I had to work, so I tried to hide it from her, but I couldn't stop her seeing some of it. I still had to get water from the well, because we needed even more with her being there because she was so hot and wanting to wash all the time.

She didn't want to go anywhere or see anything while she was there, she just wanted to stay with Nadia and me in the house. All the local women wanted to look at her

130

and the house was always full while she was there. She could never get used to the way they all spat in public and chewed *qat*. Some women travelled a long way to meet her, and told her how terrible they thought it was that she should have lost her daughters in this way.

Mo used to get so angry about what had happened to us. He wanted to kill everyone. He wanted to kill Dad and Abdul Khada.

I had to go to the shops more often than normal in order to get fresh food for them. While Mum was with me Salama allowed Nadia to come to stay with us, but when Mum went to Nadia's for the second week I wasn't allowed to go with them.

Mum was suffering all the time from the flies and mosquitoes, all the things which Nadia and I had grown used to over the previous five or six years were like a nightmare to her. We were able to use the new room on the roof for her, and I thought she might be more comfortable there, but it was just as bad. She was feeling sick all the time and Mo was coming out in rashes all over his body from the mosquito bites. After two weeks Nadia and I couldn't handle the strain of it any longer. 'The quicker you go Mum,' I said, 'the quicker we'll be able to get out of here. Don't worry about us, we have waited this long, we can wait a bit longer for you to arrange something.' She said that it made her feel so helpless to do anything for us, but she agreed that it would be best if she got back to England and contacted more people.

We arranged a taxi for her through Amina's son-in-law, and on the morning it arrived I walked down the hill to the road with them. Nadia said she couldn't face the emotional strain of this final parting and she had said goodbye to them the night before.

When we got to the road Mum told me not to worry, she would get the tape publicised. I saw them both into the car and said goodbye, walking all the way back to my room without looking back once. I thought if I turned

131

round and saw the car driving off into the desert with my Mum inside it my heart would break.

When I got to my room I was exhausted. I collapsed on the bed and all my emotions burst out in torrents of sobbing and tears.

Abdul Khada had decided that he couldn't trust us to be with Mum in the village, and he came down from Saudi to make sure nothing was happening. He had expected Mum to stay for several months and he was shocked to hear that she was already in Taiz, preparing to fly home. He went to see her in town and realised from what she said, and the fact that she was flying back to England so quickly, that she was going to try to do something to save us. He told her to forget it, that there was nothing she could do, and to leave us alone. She took no notice of him.

He came out to Hockail that night with Mohammed and by the time he got there he was boiling with anger and certain that he was being betrayed. He wanted to know exactly what we had told her and what was going on.

'Nothing,' I said. 'It's none of your business any more.' I knew I shouldn't say any more but I couldn't resist going on, I felt so sure that we were finally going to get out. 'I'm not stopping here any longer, I'm going home now.'

He slapped me across the face with his hand. 'You are lucky you are carrying that baby inside you,' he shouted, 'or I would be hitting you much harder.'

'If your Mum wants you back,' Mohammed told me, 'she will have to pay for you, just like we had to. That's the rule in this country.' I took no notice and they kept on teasing me.

As the time of my delivery drew closer I realised that there was no chance Abdul Khada would let me back to England for the birth. Mum's visit meant that he certainly didn't trust me now. I had to face the frightening prospect of giving birth in the village, just like Nadia and Bakela.

Two days later my waters broke while I was in the house on my own. I was shocked by how much of it there was. I was dressed at the time, so I changed my trousers and took the soiled ones up onto the roof to wash. I started getting nagging pains in my back, and I found I had soaked another pair of trousers without realising. I had no idea what would happen next, but I knew we needed water in the tanks for the day, so I set out to the well. By the time I got back with the water on my head the pains were getting bad and I went back up onto the roof to rest.

Ward came up and found me sitting there alone and asked what was wrong. I told her the pains were getting bad and that my waters had broken. She called Abdul Khada and they took me downstairs to my room. I was very frightened of what was coming, although the pains themselves were not that bad compared to what I had been through since arriving in the Yemen.

Gradually the pains increased and I started to cry. Saeeda came into the room to soothe me, and Ward was in there too. I kept pacing around the room, unable to stay still. It was about ten at night by then, so the room was lit by the smoky, paraffin lamps. After midnight I lay down on the floor and couldn't move around any more. I started pushing at about two o'clock in the morning. Ward had fallen asleep. I woke her up and told her the baby was coming. She told me not to be stupid, that it wouldn't be coming until the next day, and to stop making such a fuss. My body told me she was wrong. I didn't argue with her, I just pulled my trousers off and kept pushing. She soon realised I was serious. She got up and walked across the room. She stood at my feet, watching to see what would happen.

Saeeda, the old lady, tied a rope to the window and gave me the other end to hold onto. I kept wanting to close my legs and Ward was getting angry and shouting

133

at me to open them. When the baby's head came through I screamed with the pain. Ward crouched down on her haunches to watch. The baby slid out and I waited for Ward to pick it up, cut the cord and show it to me as I had seen her do with Bakela. But she stayed down there, doing something between my legs, and I couldn't tell what was happening. She called Abdul Khada to bring in a torch and hold it for her because the lamp didn't give her enough light to work by.

'What are you doing?' I shouted.

'The cord is round its neck,' she replied, without looking up. 'I'm undoing it.' A few moments later she freed the baby, cut the cord, and slapped it, making it cry. It was a boy.

Abdul Khada was delighted, 'So,' he said, 'now we have our souvenir. We don't need you any more. You can go back to England.' He laughed and I knew that he was just taunting me. He still had no intention of letting me go. If I had thought he meant it I would have gone immediately.

Ward covered me up on the floor. I couldn't move. The afterbirth hadn't come out, but I didn't know anything about that. When dawn broke Ward told me to stand up. She tied a piece of string around the end of the cord which was still hanging out of me, and tied it to my leg. I found out that they always do that because they believe that if they don't the cord is going to go back inside and then the afterbirth will never come out.

They made me stay standing up, waiting for it to come out. I felt dizzy and weak with tiredness, and kept staggering on my feet, but they forced me back up again. In the end I couldn't stand any more and I had to lie down. Ward went down to the village to get a woman to help get the afterbirth out of me. By that time Amina and Haola had come up to help as well.

A woman from the village arrived and made me stand up again. She started squeezing my belly. The pain was worse than the birth itself as she tried to force it out by digging her fingers into me. She seemed worried that it wasn't coming and I began to panic. After half an hour of agony it finally slid out. It was more of a relief than the birth itself. I suddenly felt clean.

The woman bathed and washed me and washed the baby. Abdul Khada brought me some food but I couldn't eat it, I just fell asleep. The next thing I knew Ward was waking me up and telling me to feed the baby. I didn't have much milk for him, but I fed him as best I could.

Ward didn't help me with anything, she wouldn't even clean my room and by the third day the dust was getting too heavy to bear, so I got up to do it for myself and I started to get on with all my other jobs as well. Looking after a baby is a lot harder when you don't have any of the modern conveniences, things which we take for granted in England. We didn't have nappies, for instance, which meant that all day long we had to clean and wash the babies, every time they wet themselves or messed. Once they started on solid foods we had to give them chopped up chapatis, soaked in milk, although when he came home Abdul Khada did sometimes bring me some jars of baby food from Saudi Arabia. Bringing up babies is hard anywhere in the world, but it is ten times as hard when you are doing it on your own with no modern inventions to help you, at the same time as all the other traditional women's chores.

They wanted to call the baby Mohammed, but I wanted something more English, so I called him Marcus. When they first handed him to me I knew that I was going to have to leave him behind when I went back to England. I knew they would never let me take him with me. I couldn't stop myself from loving him, but I knew he was never going to be mine, not really.

CHAPTER TWELVE
Someone Out There Cares

Marcus was born on 8 May 1986. It was almost as if he knew that one day I would have to leave him. He would cling to me all the time, because he didn't have anyone else. There were only Ward and the two old people in the house with me, so he stayed by my side all the time, even if I went down to the shops. I did my best to be a good mother. He was a good baby, hardly ever crying as long as I was around to hold him.

My milk dried up within a couple of weeks and Abdul Khada brought me some bottles of powdered milk from Taiz. The milk made Marcus very sick for a few days, he brought it back up every time I fed him, but eventually he adjusted to it.

Abdul Khada immediately loved his new grandson and he used to send me clothes for Marcus from Saudi. I think he thought he had finally defeated me, that I would never go back to England now that I had Marcus. I didn't say anything, but I kept my resolve. I had to get back home. I was relieved that the baby was a boy because I knew that when I did leave him he would be all right. If it had been a girl I would have been frightened about what would happen to her without me there to protect her.

About a month after Marcus was born I received a big envelope from England with 'happy birthday' written on it. I knew it must be from Mum, so before I opened it I sent for Nadia to come. When she arrived we opened the envelope together and found two application forms for British passports. We didn't know what Mum was planning at that stage, but we filled them in and sent them back to her through the doctor. Mum had provided another big envelope for us to send them back in, and we wrote 'happy sixteenth birthday' on the outside and addressed it to our sister in England. We felt elated, laughing hysterically as we filled the forms in, at last something seemed to be happening.

The letter got through and Mum wrote back to say she had received the forms and everything was going fine. It finally looked as if we were getting somewhere. All we had to do now was wait and hope. But then Mum realised that we needed recent photographs for the passports. She asked us if we could get into Taiz to have some taken. I couldn't believe that having seen how we were kept in the village, she thought we could just go down into Taiz when we wanted to. Suddenly it looked as if all the steps we had taken forward were to no purpose.

Nadia had her baby Tina a couple of weeks after I had Marcus, but it didn't go as smoothly as before. Like the first time, I didn't know anything about it until after it was all over. I went down to Ashube on the morning after she had had it. When I walked into the house I was looking around for a new born baby and I saw one that looked about six months old. She had long black hair and she seemed to be staring straight at me already.

'Where's your baby?' I asked.

'This is her,' Nadia replied.

I was shocked. 'How did you give birth to something so huge?' I asked.

She told me that she was in labour for three days, but no-one had come up to tell me about it. I think Nadia deliberately stopped me from knowing because she knew how worried I would be. On the third day she started pushing, and it went on for six hours, but the baby wouldn't move. She told me that she was screaming all the way through, and the other women said they were sure she was going to die. None of them thought she could live through such a terrible birth. They were all terrified.

After six hours an old woman from the village came in. She was one of the women who did the circumcising for the girls. She saw how desperately Nadia was struggling, she picked up a used razor blade which was lying on the side, and cut her down below without even washing it. The moment she made the cut the baby came free and was born.

The woman said that she had to do something fast or either the mother or the baby would have died. I asked Nadia how she felt and she said she was really sore. She never saw a doctor or had any medical treatment at all. The women had gone to get a doctor from the other side of Ashube when it looked as if Nadia would die, but by the time he got there the old woman had done the job and so he left again without examining her. The doctor who had been helping us with the letters could easily have helped her, but the women wouldn't allow a local man to be that intimate with a girl.

One woman in the village, who was actually a cousin of the doctor, had a breech birth in which the baby died inside her with just its legs hanging out. The doctor was eventually told and ran to the house but it was much too late. He asked his cousin and the women around her why they hadn't come for him earlier, because if they had he could have saved the baby's life. They told him they were too ashamed to come to a man for help in such a matter.

I used to ask the doctor questions when I went to see him, and he always tried to answer me honestly. I think he was very shy, and he wasn't used to talking to local women about anything personal. When I asked him what was wrong with me and why I got the pains in my chest, he told me it was stress, and that was what the tablets were for.

They circumcised Nadia's new baby, Tina, on the fourth day, which was traditional for the girls, although the boys were done after seven days, if they were strong and healthy enough.

Not long afterwards Marcus started to become ill. He began to cry and he just wouldn't stop. He vomited and wouldn't take any food. I didn't know what to do because the doctor was away travelling again. He cried solidly for 48 hours. I kept him with me all the time and no-one else seemed to take any notice of us during the day. During the nights Ward would come in and accuse me of doing things to him to keep him awake and make him unhappy. I just told her to get out of my room and leave us alone. All I could do was hold him and try to comfort him. I became very frightened for him, and as I grew more tired I became more desperate.

By the third day of no sleep I couldn't stand it any more. Abdul Noor was at home then. I went to him and told him that I had to get Marcus to the hospital. If he didn't help me, I said, I would hire a car and go myself. I doubt if anyone would have agreed to take me, but I said it just the same, and he could see that I wasn't going to back down. He agreed to come with me.

Early next morning we set out for Taiz with Marcus, who was still crying. Abdul Noor knew of a children's hospital and we went straight there. As we walked in we were met by a wall of noise, mostly from the children waiting to be seen, crying and moaning. Rows of benches were filled with mothers and fathers holding their kids, looking lost and desperate. We joined them on the wooden benches. Some of the children were badly injured and bleeding from car accidents, or had serious burns, but there was no-one to help them until it was their turn to be seen. Marcus and I sat there for hours as Abdul Noor went round the hospital trying in vain to find someone to see us. Marcus continued to cry all the

139

time. I thought we would never get in to see anyone qualified to help.

We finally got in to see a doctor who listened to what I said, but he didn't give me any explanation, he just handed me some medicine and told me to give it to Marcus. He didn't say anything else and he was obviously ready to see the next patient, so we had to leave. We got straight back into the taxi and returned to the village.

I gave Marcus the medicine and he got a bit better, at least it stopped his crying, but he continued to be a sickly child, not eating and staying skinny and weak. Ward kept telling me that he was just like his father had been at that age, and I hated the thought that he might turn out to be like Abdullah.

Some months before Tina was born rumours had begun to go round that Salama, Nadia's mother-in-law, was going to join Gowad in England. Gowad had been trying for two years to get her a visa to travel there, and now she had a health problem which meant she needed to travel to England for treatment. Salama was very keen to go, she always said how much she missed Gowad when he was away; by then she hadn't seen him for about four years. She said that she didn't want to leave Nadia, but that if she could just go to England to get better she would come straight back.

From being just a rumour it suddenly became reality and Salama was on her way. Gowad wrote to Nadia telling her not to worry and that Salama would be straight back, but Nadia was still left on her own in the house, pregnant with Tina and looking after Haney, plus Salama's two children who were about nine and four at that stage. Nadia was brilliant with children but it was a big struggle for her. The local village women helped her in any way they could, like carrying water and looking after the baby when it came. But she was still coping on her own most of the time. The little girl, Magida, was

140

good, but the nine-year-old boy, Shiab, was terrible to her. He was naughty all the time and never listened to her. He would never help her with the other children or with keeping the house tidy, and would even bite her if she tried to tell him off.

I wanted to help her myself, but I was stopped more and more by Ward from going to see Nadia. She believed I was neglecting my work in the house and she would tell Abdul Khada everything I did, in letters written for her by other people. At one stage he stopped me for several months from going to Ashube. He would threaten me in his letters to make sure I obeyed him, and I was terrified of being beaten any more when he got back, and embarrassed to think other people would know he was hitting me. So I only saw Nadia when she was able to come up and visit me. Her visits became less frequent because she had such a hard time looking after all the children. In the end Abdul Khada relented and said I could go down to her house once a month, but I couldn't be much help to her like that. We were being made to work harder than ever, and had become even more like slaves. It was as if Mum had never been out to see us: we were still trapped and helpless.

Gowad kept writing letters to Nadia telling her what was happening to Salama, but he wasn't telling her the truth. He told her that soon Salama would be coming back to the Yemen and Nadia and Mohammed would be able to go to England with their children. At the time Mohammed was still going back and forth to Saudi, spending a year there and then coming home for a few months. At least when he was at home he was able to control his little brother, Shiab, a bit, which was what Nadia needed more than anything.

Nadia seemed to believe Gowad's promises about going to England at first, but as the months went on it became obvious that Salama wasn't going to be coming back to the Yemen, and Nadia wasn't going anywhere. I soon realised that what Gowad was doing was trying to

141

get Salama a British passport like his, and he had no intention of keeping his promises to Nadia.

Nadia had always been quite close to Salama when she was there, and when she finally realised what was happening she felt betrayed, and hated Salama and Gowad for what they had done to her. They always left her short of money. Some days when I saw her she would be crying because they hadn't sent her any money to buy food and she didn't know what to do. She would have to go round the village borrowing money and food to keep things going. I told her to run a bill up in the shop and leave it to them to take care of. She didn't like the idea but in the end she had to. The shopkeepers didn't mind, they knew the situation. She also started making clothes for people on her sewing machine, like her neighbour, and letting them pay her for the work. There was never a moment when she wasn't working.

Friends who went up to Saudi would tell Mohammed off for letting his wife struggle so badly, and eventually he started sending home more money for her. There wasn't much else he could do, because he couldn't force his mother to return, or influence his father into making Nadia's life better.

Mohammed was a better husband and father than Abdullah. When Abdullah came back from Saudi and saw our son for the first time he showed no interest at all. Perhaps he felt Marcus had been forced on him, just as I did. He never wanted to stay in with us, he wanted to be out all the time. He was more like a kid himself still. Not that I wanted him around. The more time he spent away from me the better as far as I was concerned. When he did come home I ignored him because I hated him so much. I had to let him have sex with me when he demanded it, but I never took any notice of him.

Marcus was just under a year old when my brother Ahmed from Marais arrived unexpectedly at the house. This was the first time I had seen him since the visit to

142

Aden the day before Nadia was due to arrive in the Yemen. Neither Abdul Khada nor Abdullah were in the country when he arrived. I was sitting in my room when Ward called me downstairs. She was standing outside the house. I came out and saw a man with her. I didn't recognise him.

'Hello,' he said, 'I'm your brother Ahmed.'

I must have been drained of emotion by then because I didn't feel anything this time. But I hugged him to show I was pleased to see him, and asked him into the house. He didn't have any luggage with him, just the clothes he was standing up in and one small bag with a change of shirt in it.

He followed me upstairs. We sat down and started asking each other questions. I told him our story and he was shocked. He said that he had had no idea of what was happening when I visited him in Marais, otherwise he would have tried to do something about it. I told him some more of my story and how unhappy I was and he began to cry for me. Then he told me more about our sister Leilah.

After being left in the Yemen by Dad, the two of them grew up together until she was married off for the first time at ten. He told me that she grew to love her husband and stayed with him for quite a few years. But the husband went away to fight in the army and was killed. The family forced her to marry a second time to someone she didn't like. Her new husband was unkind to her and hit her. He took her to Aden to live and she now had three children and was pregnant with a fourth. Ahmed hadn't seen her for years but he heard about her from other people. Leilah must have been a fighter like me – perhaps it's Mum's blood in us – because she wasn't willing to put up with everything this man did to her.

In Aden, Ahmed told me, the women have the right to take their husbands to court if they don't think they are being treated right. Leilah did that and the court told her husband that if he didn't treat her better she would be granted a divorce. Ahmed said that after that he was kinder to her and now they got on quite well.

After we had talked for a while he fell into an exhausted sleep. He woke up later in the night and I made him something to eat and we talked about Mum. He didn't remember her at all, and he had no photographs of the family. I showed him some which Mum had given me. He talked about our Dad and how much he hated him and how terrible the things he had done to us all were. Ahmed had had letters from him in the past but hadn't replied to them. He asked me if I knew why Dad had done what he did to his children, but I didn't have any answers. He told me how he hated the army now and wanted to get out.

The fact that he had turned up unexpectedly just after Mum had gone made me suspicious, and I wondered if he had been sent by Abdul Khada or Dad to find out what was happening. I didn't want to tell him everything. By that stage I had learnt not to trust anyone. The only people I knew were on my side were Nadia and Mum, and even then I felt that it was up to me to keep pushing them to fight.

He stayed with me for about three days and it was nice to have someone friendly around the house. Nadia came up to meet him for the first time ever, the day after he arrived. He was shocked by the way Nadia and I both had to work. He said that the sort of tasks we were being asked to do were out of date, and that hardly anyone still behaved like that any more. He talked about my Grandad and about how he and Leilah felt when Dad first left them in Marais. He said he could still remember that day, with Dad leaving and he and Leilah screaming after him. He said that he couldn't remember much after that for a few years. When Grandad remarried he had more children with his second wife, and they treated Ahmed and Leilah very badly.

Ahmed believed that because Grandad hated Dad, he took his feelings out on the boy who had been left with

144

him. I began to see the stooped, grey-haired old man I met in Marais in a different light.

Ahmed went on to spend a couple of days with Nadia in Ashube and the villagers began to get suspicious of his motives. There were rumours circulating that he had come to get us out, but I knew that there was nothing he could do, he had no power to help us, he was just like us really, a prisoner of his life in the Yemen. Abdul Khada got to hear that he was there and became alarmed. He sent letters to me and to Ahmed warning us not to do anything, but at the same time he also sent me money to buy food for our guest, like a perfect host. Ahmed felt bad that he hadn't brought any food with him from the city because we were very short of fruit at the time, it had been a long time since I had tasted an orange or an apple. He promised to come back with fruit in a few weeks.

While Ahmed was staying with us, a woman from Nadia's village came up to the house. She told me that Mum had come again with some English people. I was taken by surprise, and with my heart in my mouth I scooped Marcus up into my arms and started for the door.

'Where are you going?' Ward shouted.

'I'm going to my sister,' I said.

'You can't, you'll get into trouble,' she warned.

'I don't care, I'm going,' I said, and I hurried down the mountain with the woman to Nadia's house. When I got there I found an English man and woman. They looked like tourists, covered in cameras. The house was full of local people trying to see what was going on. There was no sign of Mum. It had been a mistake. I was disappointed that she wasn't there. Nadia came up to me and spoke quietly.

'They are reporters, they've come from England to get us.'

I felt suddenly elated, but confused because Mum had led me to believe that the first people to get to us would

145

be the people from Mr Cantwell's charity in Geneva. To know that the British press were there made my spirits soar. There was no way that they could witness our lives at first hand and not raise the alarm back in Britain. It looked as if Mum had managed to find a way to get us out.

CHAPTER THIRTEEN

Facing The Dangers

The woman was Eileen Macdonald, a journalist from the *Observer* newspaper in London. The man was Ben Gibson, a photographer who was travelling with her on our story. They also had a woman interpreter with them – it was her whom the local women had mistaken for Mum – and a driver. The driver had a pistol tucked into his belt which he was fingering nervously. Some of the men who were around the room had guns as well.

I went straight over to Eileen and spoke to her. 'We have been waiting for you,' I said. 'Are you going to take us out? I beg you to take us with you.' I thought they had finally come to free us.

She seemed very calm and quiet. I warned her to be careful what she said because a lot of the men in the room spoke English.

Eileen spoke to the driver. 'Is there any way we can take the girls and their children back to Taiz in the jeep?'

The driver looked worried. Apparently they hadn't told him they were journalists. He was driving a UNICEF jeep and believed they were doctors wanting to visit us while on holiday because they were friends of Mum's. The gleaming white jeep was well known in the mountain villages because it brought medical supplies to a little clinic in the centre of Mokbana. No-one ever gave them any trouble. Ahmed had been telling the driver our story while Nadia and I were talking to Eileen, and although he wanted to help, he was frightened of what would happen to him if he did. Eileen and Ben had told him they had presents for us from our family. The man shook his head and talked back quickly and quietly to the interpreter.

'I can't take these girls, I'm known in these parts. If I took them the men from round here would hunt me down. They know I work at the hospital in Taiz, they would find me easily. It would be suicide for all of us to try to take them away like this. They would never let us out of the mountains anyway.'

More men were in the room by now and one of them started shouting that they could take Nadia and me but they could not take the children. We were both holding our babies in our arms.

I became mad and started shouting. 'All right then, I'll leave the boy. I was raped to get him anyway. I will leave him.'

Nadia tried to restrain me. She looked so unhappy. She knew how much I wanted to get away, and she wanted to just as much, but she couldn't bear the thought of leaving her children. Haney was staring around at all the grown-ups, with a bewildered look on his face.

The men all began to shout at once, and some of them got to their feet, shaking their fists. The driver's hand went to his gun. The translator warned Eileen that things were getting too heated, and suggested that they hand round some of the *qat* which they had brought with them. Eileen was obviously relieved to have something to defuse the situation. It was passed round and the men all calmed down as they began chewing.

'Is there anywhere private we can go?' Eileen asked me.

'Yeah, come with me,' I said, and she, Ben, Nadia and I went outside. I led them down the mountain to squat at the back of one of the other houses, beneath a sheer cliff face. It would be harder for anyone to overhear us there.

'We thought everyone had forgotten us,' I said. 'We have been waiting seven years for someone to save us, and we thought you were the ones.'

'I'm sorry.' Eileen seemed genuinely upset by our situation; she was obviously a brave woman to have got this far. 'I don't think we are going to be able to do it just like that. On this trip we only expected to talk to you, not to rescue you. I think we are going to have to go away and get more official help.'

She went on to tell us how everyone had tried to dissuade them from coming into the mountain villages of the Mokbana area. People in Taiz had told her how the men of the villages were just bandits, who would think nothing of killing a stranger who seemed to be nosing around. Apparently they tried to take a population census of the whole of the Yemen a few years before, but all the information gatherers who came up into the Mokbana area asking questions had disappeared, never to be seen again. Eileen and Ben had been told that no-one travels in the mountain districts without a gun, even if they are only going for a picnic.

She had been shocked by how hard it was to find anyone who knew where the villages were, and by how rough the roads were. Even coming in a Land Rover they had to travel most of the way at five miles an hour.

'I couldn't believe how the scenery changed,' she told me later, 'from a stream with green trees and kingfishers on the banks, we were suddenly into barren mountain landscapes.'

Once they were into the mountains they began to meet people who had heard about us. They told her that we were known as 'the poor, sad sisters of Mokbana', because we were always crying. They told her we wanted to go home but that the men would never let us. Everyone up there knew about our story.

As they got closer to our villages they found people who actually knew us personally, and someone told them that Nadia's house was the one with the yellow-painted

149

door and windows. Until that moment they hadn't known if they would ever actually find us.

Although she had been warned about how impossible it would be to get us out she had gone on believing that she could in the end, even if not on this visit. Now she realised just how hard it would be. She explained that if we went with her now we would be stopped at the roadblocks and asked for our papers. Neither Nadia nor I had any identification papers. If the word got around that they had come to rescue us, they would be shot before they could get back to the main road, she realised that. There were also rumours of an army camp in the mountains not far from the villages, and Eileen had been warned that word of their arrival would soon spread to the soldiers, who would have no hesitation in shooting first and asking questions later.

What we didn't know then was that almost at the time we were talking, Gowad was telephoning the Commander of the villages, warning him that there were two dangerous journalists in Mokbana working as spies and looking for ways to cause trouble. The Commander was promising Gowad that he would take action immediately. He considered sending a squad of police up to the villages to arrest the journalists that afternoon, then decided it was too late and that they could go in the cool of dawn. If Gowad had made his call a day earlier, Eileen and Ben would have walked straight into an ambush.

In England the publicity was rumbling on, but the *Birmingham Post* was running a story with the headline: 'Yemeni sisters face little hope of help.' This was a report of a meeting between Roy Hattersley, Mum's local MP, and the Yemeni Ambassador in London.

Meanwhile, back in the mountains, unaware of these developments, Eileen was firing questions at us, trying to get as much of our story out of us as she could before someone else came out to disturb us. We told her as much as we could think of. She had brought us a letter

150

from Mum, and she told us everything that Mum had been doing. Apparently my tape had been played to reporters who had cried when they heard it, and some of it had been broadcast on the radio. What she didn't tell me, but I found out later, was that many of the papers had run some bits of the story, concentrating on the idea of 'Sex Slave Sisters', and only talking about how we were forced to sleep with Abdullah and Mohammed, ignoring all the rest. Apparently Mum had been badly upset by that.

Mum's first contact had been a man called Alf Dickens, who introduced her to a journalist on the *Birmingham Post* called Tom Quirke. Tom listened to the tape I had made and read our letters, and decided it was the biggest story his paper had ever had.

He went to see Dad to get his side of it, and Dad told him that he had been unhappy about our behaviour in England and had wanted us to learn from the Yemen's traditional Muslim culture. The paper's lawyers were worried about accusing Dad of selling us at first, so the story appeared on the front page of how we had disappeared under 'mysterious circumstances'.

On the day that story appeared, Alf Dickens and Mum held a press conference. The journalists who came along seemed not to believe Mum at that stage, but Tom Quirke contacted the *Observer* and the story was given to Eileen to follow up.

I couldn't bear the thought of Eileen and Ben just going away and leaving us again. I was desperate to think up a plan which would allow us to go with them immediately. I was talking and thinking at the same time. 'What if we told them that Mum was in Taiz, too sick to cross the mountains, and she has sent you to get us, so that she can see her grandchildren before she dies?'

Somehow, in the atmosphere of desperation it seemed as if a mad story like that might just work, and we decided to try it. The men were starting to come out of the house and hanging around listening to our conversation, so we went back inside with the others and Nadia and I explained to them about our mother and the illness story.

One of the eldest men nodded wisely. 'First we will send someone to Taiz to see how sick your mother is. Then if it is true, he will come back and take you for a visit.'

We had to think quickly now. I asked Eileen if her newspaper couldn't fly Mum in and put her in a hospital in Taiz, but I could already see that it was all too wild to work. Ahmed was also coming up with wild ideas of his own about coming back with some of his army friends the next day, shooting it out with the men and just driving away with us. I could tell it wasn't going to work, but I was desperate for something to happen. I was beginning to realise that yet again we were going to be left behind while the people who had come to save us drove off on their own. Eileen promised that as soon as they got to Sana'a they would go to the British Embassy. She promised that help would be coming soon, but that we must be patient.

'What do you think we have been doing for the last seven years?' I asked, sarcastically. 'Patience is one thing we are perfect at.'

'Don't worry,' Eileen said, 'it will just be a matter of weeks before you are out of here now.'

'Try not to antagonise the villagers by telling them all the time you are going to leave,' the interpreter warned me. 'If you keep telling them that they may move you to an even more remote village and no-one will be able to find you at all.'

'We can't keep quiet about leaving here,' I exploded, 'it's the only thing we talk and dream about. We only keep sane by saying it over and over again.'

By the time Ben and Eileen left, the whole village was there to see them go, the children running ahead as they stumbled down the crumbling mountain path to the

Land Rover. Nadia and I were both crying by the time they went. We were so confused, because it had all happened so fast.

Later I heard that they were stopped twice by roadblocks and armed men wanting to know what they were doing up there, and searching to see if they were trying to smuggle us out. There was no doubt that they had taken their lives in their hands coming this far. To us Eileen seemed like an angel sent from heaven.

Once we had got over the initial disappointment of not going with them we felt much more optimistic about the future. We felt that now there really was some hope. We put all our trust in Eileen.

Ahmed joined them in Taiz and they started by going to the director of the hospital who had lent them the jeep, and who had offered to contact Muhsen Al Usifi, the Governor of Taiz, on their behalf before they set off into the mountains. The Governor, however, had been away in Sana'a then, and still wasn't back.

'I promise you,' the director assured them, 'the Governor will be told about this as soon as he returns to Taiz, and the girls will be brought down into the city for questioning.'

He went on to tell Eileen: 'If the Governor wishes it, then they can go home to their mother at once. If he wants to hear the husbands' side, then they will be recalled to Taiz from Saudi Arabia, and there will be a court case. The girls must then ask for divorces. It will cost lots of money and could take five years. Everyone has to be bribed – from the soldiers who go into Mokbana to fetch them to the lawyers and the judges.'

Eileen and Ben then flew down to Sana'a, with the National Security forces close behind them, and made contact with Jim Halley, a new consul at the Embassy who was helping them. He met them at the airport and took them to the British Ambassador in a bullet-proof, riot-proof jeep.

They arrived at the heavy metal gates. Jim sounded his

horn and an armed guard opened a small door in the gates and scrutinised them, and the gates swung open.

Eileen's approach to these people was as aggressive as mine. She went on at the Ambassador about our problems, and he tried to find the right officials to talk to. Because they were worried that the National Security forces were right behind them, Eileen and Ben asked to stay the night inside the guarded embassy.

Ben had to get his pictures back to England to appear in that Sunday's *Observer*, and he smuggled Eileen's story out with him, after she had sat up most of the night writing it.

The Ambassador and Jim felt it was important that they got Eileen out of the Yemen before the story appeared in the paper in England. If she was still in the country then, she might well be arrested as soon as she tried to leave, and thrown in prison. In the end they managed to get her on a flight on Saturday night.

When Eileen arrived at London's Heathrow Airport her fiancé, Paul, was waiting with a copy of that morning's *Observer*. Her story was on the front page, with a picture taken by Ben of Nadia holding Tina in her arms. We were famous.

CHAPTER FOURTEEN

A Saviour Appears

Soon after Eileen left Mokbana the rumours began to spread. Everyone now knew that they were reporters travelling under false pretences, but by the time people realised what had happened Eileen and Ben were safely back in Britain. If they had been caught I don't know what would have happened to them. If they had still been in the mountains they would probably have been shot. If they had been caught in Taiz or Sana'a they would probably have been imprisoned and accused of attempted kidnap. They might well have ended up being executed.

When we realised that everyone now knew who they were we became very frightened that they might not have made it out of the Yemen in time. We had no way of knowing what was happening in Taiz, let alone Sana'a or London. We had seen them leave but we had no way of knowing what had happened after that, whether the tide of rumour and anger had caught up with them, or whether they had managed to stay ahead of it all the way to their plane.

We were kept in the dark, until a letter arrived from Mum, telling us what Eileen had been doing since getting back to Britain. Suddenly, she told us, the whole thing had exploded all over the world. Eileen had written a long article about her meeting with us in the village and everyone was now interested. The governments were involved and being forced to take us seriously. After seven years of crying in the dark, the world's spotlight was suddenly turned on us, although nothing changed in Mokbana and we only heard about what was happening second-hand.

Earlier, in her attempts to rescue us, Mum had approached Roy Hattersley, who was her local MP and the Shadow Home Secretary, to ask for help. The first time nothing had happened, but the second time he started to badger the government, and talked to Sir Geoffrey Howe, who was the Foreign Secretary at the time, and Douglas Hurd, who was Home Secretary, about our situation. The British Government had wanted to hush it up, they certainly hadn't wanted to have reporters stirring things up between them and the Yemeni Government. Now it was too late for them to do any covering up, the whole world was finding out what had happened to us from an eyewitness, with pictures to back her story up.

Abdul Khada, as always, had managed to find out what was going on quicker than anyone else, even though he was in Saudi Arabia. He always seemed to be able to get information about things the moment they happened. He must have had sources everywhere who contacted him about everything that happened in the Yemen and in Britain. The Yemeni men all deal in rumour and gossip, and news travels very fast because so many of them move around from country to country. He immediately wrote me a letter telling me that he knew there had been reporters in the villages and assuring me that there was nothing they could do, and God help me, he threatened, if they tried anything.

For the first time I realised that I wasn't frightened of him now. I didn't care about any of them any more. There was nothing further I felt they could do to hurt me. All I could think about now was my freedom, and I felt confident that sooner or later something was going to happen.

156

Our brother Ahmed came to visit us again whilst on leave from the army, but this time he had a lot of trouble reaching us. The villagers had told the police that he was a troublemaker and a thief, and that several things had gone missing from the villages during his previous visit. They were all very wary of anyone who looked as if they might want to help us, and they did their best to stop him getting to us. He arrived first at Ashube and the village men met him. They told him Abdul Khada had found out he was on his way and had sent a telegram saying that he could say 'hello' to us but then he must leave straight away, and they were going to make sure that he obeyed. They told him that if he tried to help us they would have him arrested. By the time he got to my house he was crying.

Abdul Noor, Abdul Khada's brother, was at home in Hockail from Saudi Arabia at that time. When he heard that Ahmed had come to my house he came up to talk to him. He was a nicer man than his brother, but he was acting on Abdul Khada's behalf. He wanted to know what Ahmed wanted and whether he thought he could take us away. I told him that Ahmed hadn't come to make any trouble and begged him to let him stay. Abdul Noor believed me and agreed.

A few days later Abdul Noor brought me another letter from Abdul Khada. He gave me the letter and showed me that he had a tape as well. I read the letter first. Abdul Khada told me that he had been sent a copy of Eileen's article from Britain, and he told me to listen to the tape. I fetched my recorder and gave it to Abdul Noor. Abdul Khada's voice came out of the speaker.

He was saying: 'All the things that I have done for you and you don't thank me for it. I thought you would have been happy by now and forgotten all about your family. I thought you would accept the fact that you were married, and then you could have gone to visit your Mum and Dad. If you want to go just let me know and I will let you go freely, but you will have to leave your son

157

with us. Your Mum is a very strong woman. It is unbelievable what she has done for her kids. I understand what she has done and you can go freely.'

I knew he still didn't believe that I would leave Marcus. He thought that he was safe in offering to let me go, that it would look as if I was staying of my own free will. He seemed to be rambling, like someone who was paranoid. One moment he was saying that Eileen's article wouldn't do me any good, that no-one would take any notice, and the next moment he was saying that I could go freely. He seemed to be threatening me one moment and making up to me the next. I was glad to hear the changes in his tone. I knew that meant the situation was finally changing and he was losing control. When the tape finished Abdul Noor took it out of the recorder and put it in his pocket.

'Can I keep that?' I asked, thinking that I could play it to other men in the village and they would have to let me go.

'No,' he shook his head, 'it is just for you to listen to.' I never saw the tape again.

I went to my room to write a reply. Knowing that he expected me to say that I wanted to stay with Marcus, I wrote instead that I wanted to leave, and asked when I could go. I knew that he wouldn't make the offer again now he knew I would accept.

I went to tell Nadia what had happened, and described the tape. She no longer seemed to be interested in anything. Eileen described Nadia's eyes as being 'dead' when she first saw her, and I suppose that was how she had become. She accepted that she was going to go home, and she knew that she was going to have to leave her children, but it was breaking her heart. I don't think she could actually bear to think about it any more, so she just cut it out and went on with her life like a zombie. They had managed to kill all the spark that had been in Nadia when she was a girl.

We agreed that if there was a chance for one of us to

get out first, we would leave our kids with the other and go to England to continue fighting to rescue the one who was left behind. I hoped that Nadia would be the first to go, because I knew that if I was left in the Yemen I would be able to go on fighting them for ever, but I didn't think she would be able to keep fighting long if I wasn't around to keep her going.

The following day Abdul Noor called to me from the roof of his house. He told me to come down. When I got there he met me outside the house.

'Somebody has come to see you,' he said.

'Who?' I asked.

'Abdul Walli,' he said. 'He is the Commander of the police. He is an important man, you must show a lot of respect for him when you go in. He has been sent by the government of Taiz to investigate your case.'

'Where is he?' I wanted to know.

'He is waiting for you in the house belonging to his wife's family.'

I had heard about him and I knew how important he was, but I had never met him. He was said to have the ear of all the top people in the country.

'What does he want to know?' I wanted to be clear about what was happening.

'He has heard about your case,' Abdul Noor said. 'Newspapers from England have reached places like Libya and Saudi Arabia. The Government wants to know what is going on, and they have asked him to find out.'

We walked down the road to the house where Abdul Walli was waiting. By this time I was expected to wear a veil whenever I was anywhere where other men might see me. There were men passing in cars on the road, so I had to maintain my modesty until I got inside the house. The house was full of people and Abdul Noor told me to go into the room with the other women and wait there.

'I'll call you when Abdul Walli is ready to see you,' he said.

The women were all dying to know what was going on and why such an important man would want to see me. They had all heard about the newspaper articles and they kept asking me questions. I just wanted to shut them up so that I could stay calm and prepare myself to meet someone who might be able to rescue us. I was as openly sarcastic and rude to them as I knew how, just to stop their questions.

A few minutes later Abdul Noor came to the door and called for me. I followed him to another room and he showed me in. It was a big room, with one man sitting alone, cross-legged on a cushion in the far corner. He was dressed like a Saudi in a long white robe, he had taken off his headdress and put it down beside him. He had some papers on a table in front of him. He was short and fat with dark, curly hair, and looked as if he was in his mid- to late-thirties. He looked important.

'Hello,' he said politely.

'Hello.'

'Please,' he gestured to the floor in front of his table, 'please sit down.'

'Please leave us,' he said to Abdul Noor, and waited while the other man left the room before continuing. 'I had no idea of what was happening to you here in the village,' he admitted. 'Will you tell me about it?'

I told the story again in rough outline. When I had finished he tried to explain to me about the customs of his country and their religion, and asked me if I had ever thought of settling down with Abdullah, and if I had ever felt I loved him at all during the years of the marriage.

'No,' I stayed firm, 'I hate him and I don't want him.' I was crying and I could see that he was upset by my emotions.

'I have already been to see your sister Nadia today,' he told me, 'and I had the same conversation with her that I am having with you now. She also tells me that she is unhappy and wants to go home to England, but she wants to take her children and husband with her. How do you

160

feel about that?'

I knew that Nadia had said that because it was the only chance she had of getting Haney and Tina out with us. If she rejected Mohammed the children would automatically stay with him. Although she hated Mohammed and Gowad as much as I hated Abdullah and Abdul Khada, she was frightened to show it in front of other people in case they took her children away from her. The men had trapped her in exactly the way they had intended. I couldn't hide my feelings like she could.

For what seemed like minutes he sat thinking in silence, and I waited respectfully, as Abdul Noor had told me. Finally he spoke.

'OK,' he said, 'you can go now. Goodbye.' I stood up and left the room. Although he hadn't said anything I was sure I knew what would happen now. I was sure that he would go back to Taiz and tell higher officials that it was true what the papers said and then we would get out. The fact that it was now nearly seven years since we had arrived in the Yemen meant that a bit more waiting wouldn't make much difference. I was excited to think that we were finally starting to talk to people with some influence, people who were far stronger than Abdul Khada and all the other village men.

I put my veil back on and left the house alone, returning home to the top of the cliff. As I passed her house Amina wanted to know what had happened, but I just told her to mind her own business and kept walking. I felt relieved, as if a great weight had been lifted off me. I had finally been able to explain my case to the people that mattered.

Ward and the old couple never mentioned anything that was going on. I suppose they felt there was nothing they could do about it, that it was out of their hands, and that if they talked to me about it I would just be insolent to them. So, no matter how much they talked about it amongst themselves, they kept quiet in front of me.

The old woman, Saeeda, had been kind to me over the

years. Because she was there every day she had seen how I had been made to suffer and work, and she used to say, 'Don't worry, child; may God be with you. If He thinks you are innocent and what has been done to you is wrong, then He will put it right.' I began to think that perhaps she was right.

I went to see Nadia and we talked about what we had said to Abdul Walli. She explained to me why she had said she wanted to go to England with Mohammed, and I felt frightened for her. She was so close to Haney and Tina, and I felt scared of what would happen if they tried to part her from them. I was still managing to block out of my mind the idea of leaving Marcus behind. It was something I was just going to have to do, so there was no point making myself suffer by thinking about it.

Haney had reached an age where he was starting to understand what was going on, and he would ask questions like 'Mummy, are you going to leave me?' To hear him made my heart feel as if it was breaking and I could imagine the effect it must be having on Nadia.

Two days later Abdul Noor came up to the house to see me. 'I have been told to take you and Nadia to the city,' he explained. 'We will leave first thing in the morning, so be ready to go.'

'What for?' I asked.

'Somebody wants to see you.'

'Will we be going in the same car?'

'Yes.'

I didn't believe that, because if it was true it would be the first time we had been allowed to travel anywhere together since Nadia had arrived in the Yemen seven years before. That in itself was exciting for me.

'What about the baby?'

'No, you will only be going for a day, so leave him here, you will be back in the evening. Be down at the bottom of the hill at five o'clock and I'll be waiting for you.'

'OK.'

I was awake all that night thinking about what was happening. Ward came into my room early in the morning to take over Marcus and to help me into my city outfit, which was the complete black cloak and veil. The cloak went to my waist, and then black skirts stretched down to the ground. I wore my normal Arab trousers underneath. It was an outfit which Abdul Khada had had made for me in Saudia Arabia. Nadia had had an identical outfit made for her in the village. By that time we had got used to the heat, even when wearing so many layers of clothing. Even when dressed formally like that we still wore rubber flip-flops on our feet since they were the only shoes that were suitable in those conditions. The thongs used to break all the time and we had to renew them virtually every month.

Once I was dressed I started on my way down the cliff face in the dark, with my skirts hitched up round my waist. Abdul Noor stood on the roof of his house shining a torch up to help me to see my footing. I was frightened of tripping up in the dark, even though I knew the path well by day. He met me at the bottom and together we went down the next hill to the Land Rover waiting on the road. It was a twelve seater, but there was no-one else travelling with us that day.

We drove to Ashube and waited for Nadia, who was also on her way down in the dark. When she arrived she climbed in and we sat together in the car. I felt exhilarated at actually going out with her. Neither of us could believe that it was happening to us. It was like a dream.

'I don't believe this,' I said. 'We aren't really going anywhere, we are just going to sit in the car for a few minutes and then someone is going to spoil it for us and tell us we have to go back to the villages, and to that horrible house.' But no-one came out to stop us, and the Land Rover started grinding and bumping over the desert roads, its headlights cutting arcs in the blackness.

As we approached Taiz the sun began to rise.

163

CHAPTER FIFTEEN

Prisoners In A Palace

We travelled non-stop to Taiz. 'Where are we actually going?' I asked Abdul Noor as we entered the city.

'We're going to somebody's house,' was all he would say. 'Somebody important.' We travelled on through the dirty, crowded streets in thoughtful silence. The men always liked to surround everything they did in mystery. I suppose they felt it gave them more power over us.

Wherever you are in Taiz you can see a mountain covered in houses towering above the main city. From down amongst the heat, noise, dust and dirt of the city-centre streets that mountain always looks serene and peaceful. The driver kept driving past the narrow back streets and we seemed to be heading straight for the mountain. Before long we reached it and began to drive upwards, so that we could see out across the roofs below.

The roads became smooth and the scenery grew beautiful. The houses looked lovely, and perfectly cared for. It was like a different world from the rest of the city, and a different planet from the villages of Mokbana. We went on driving round the graceful bends, past high walls which gave us occasional glimpses into beautiful gardens, looking at one grand house after another, until we turned into the street which was our destination.

From the end of the road we could see the most beautiful house of all, built into the mountain just above us, and surrounded by a high wall. It looked like a little red palace to us, with rainbow-coloured glass windows. As we came closer the wall began to obscure the building and we finally stopped in front of massive, steel gates.

Abdul Noor climbed out of the car and pressed an intercom button beside the gates. A uniformed and armed Yemeni policeman came to answer the call. Abdul Noor introduced himself and the policeman opened the gates, allowing us to drive through and park outside the main part of the house.

Nadia and I climbed the steps to a giant white, wooden door. The door was swung open by a woman in the same traditional Arab clothes as us, and we were ushered in. As we came in there was a door on the right which I assumed led to the main living room. We were led past that to another door straight ahead, and then through into yet another huge room, filled with sofas and chairs. There were curtains at the windows and wallpaper on the walls. There were dressing tables scattered around the walls and a huge colour television was flickering in the corner with the sound turned off. We had never seen such luxury.

We were invited to sit down and take off our veils. The woman offered us tea or coffee; we asked for pop. She introduced herself as Abdul Walli's wife and told us that this was one of her husband's homes. I had never met her before, even though she came from Hockail originally. She was a small woman, less than five foot tall, very pretty, and expensively dressed. She gave us our drinks and disappeared.

There was a knock on the door and Abdul Walli came in. He was still wearing the white robe which he had had on the first time I had met him. Abdul Noor followed him into the room.

'Hello.' Abdul Walli smiled pleasantly. 'I expect you are wondering what is going on. I have put your case to the Governor of Taiz and he has asked that you come up to the city to see if we can sort out your problem.'

I didn't have many questions at that stage, I just stayed

quiet to see what would happen. The men disappeared again and we stayed for a few hours in the room with Abdul Walli's wife and her housemaid, who helped her look after her baby boy. She explained that outside the front of the house was where all her husband's policemen met and chewed their *qat* at certain times of the day. She told us what a busy man her husband was and how he was hardly ever at home. She asked if I had ever met any of her family in the village, but I never had. The only time I had been to her house was on the day Abdul Walli came to talk to me. She was obviously hoping that I would bring her news of her relations, all I could say was that I had heard they were OK.

She left us on our own for a while, and then returned with the maid to give us lunch in the same room. They laid a tablecloth on the floor and then set out a meal with plates and forks. I have never seen so much food in all my life. There was rice, beef, chicken, sandwiches, soups, fruit and a variety of cakes which I had never tasted before. The four of us ate quietly together, and then Nadia and I helped them to clear up. Once the meal had been tidied away we sat down for a rest until the two men came back. By then it was the evening.

'You will be staying with us tonight,' Abdul Walli told us.

'What about the children?' I asked. I knew that Nadia had left Haney and Tina with a neighbour whom she trusted.

'Don't worry about the children,' he assured us. 'You stay here tonight.'

There was something about his confidence and his manner which made us trust him. We assumed we would be going back the next day, so we settled down and watched television for the rest of the evening. It was like arriving in paradise. Later Abdul Walli invited us through into another, even more splendid room, which I guessed was his own private sitting room. I saw a telephone, something which I hadn't seen for years.

'Is that real?' I asked, unable to believe my eyes.

'Yes,' he smiled, 'it is real.'

'Can you just pick it up and ring anywhere?'

'Yes.'

All I could think about was picking it up and ringing home to Mum. We stayed there talking to him for a while on his own and I could hardly take my eyes off the phone. He talked about Mum and what she had done, telling us all he knew about the British papers and the stories they were printing. Abdul Noor had gone back to the village to warn them that we weren't coming back that night. He had had no idea that we would be staying in Taiz when we set out that morning; Abdul Walli had only just told him. He enjoyed keeping secrets and building mysteries as well.

'You still want to leave the country do you?' he asked me conversationally.

'Yes, I want to go home.'

'Supposing,' he said pleasantly, 'you could live in the city here, would that make any difference to your feelings?'

'No,' I repeated, 'I just want to go home.'

He went on to talk generally for a while, but then came back to the same question. 'But if you could live here in the city, with your children, wouldn't that be good enough?' He asked exactly the same thing several times until I began to become tense, angry and aggressive again.

'Can't you get it through your thick head,' I snapped. 'I want to go home. I don't want to stop here. I want my Mum to continue doing what she is doing until we can go.'

He nodded and thought for a moment, then began to patiently explain how Mum's actions in going after publicity had embarrassed the Yemeni Government and how they were becoming angry.

'I don't care,' I said sulkily. 'We need publicity. People have to know what's going on. We want to go

167

home and nobody can hold us against our wills. I've gone this far and I'm not going to give up for the sake of a bit of luxury in the city.'

'Do you agree with your sister?' he asked Nadia.

'Yes, I agree with her,' Nadia said.

I wasn't going to let him wear me down with his arguments. In the last seven years I had grown too used to arguing and fighting with Yemeni men. I knew the way their minds worked and I wasn't going to let them get away with it any more. They always seemed to end up getting their own way by just refusing to listen or to take any notice of you. I knew that we were getting close to escaping and I wasn't going to give up now. It was infuriating to see the telephone and know that Mum was so close in one way, and yet we still couldn't get to her.

That night Nadia and I slept on mats on the floor of the sitting room where we had spent the day. It was carpeted and quite comfortable. The next day nothing seemed to happen and we were left hanging round the house. We were beginning to get bored. We wanted things to keep moving. We were beginning to worry about the children. I asked Abdul Walli what was happening when he finally came in to talk to us.

'We will bring the children to you here,' he assured us.

'When?' I demanded. 'We want the children now.'

'They will be here within the next two days,' he assured me.

'Fair enough,' I said.

'We just need you to sign a letter for us.'

He began asking me questions again. How had I got on with Ward? I told him how we hated each other, and how badly she had treated me, making me work from dawn till late at night, doing jobs that were mostly unnecessary. He seemed to be listening and understanding what I was saying. After a while he went out of the room. All through the day he would pop in to talk to us for a few minutes and then go off to talk to his policemen or to get on with his own business.

On the third day I started trying to get more information out of him about what was going to happen next, expecting him to try to avoid answering my questions directly.

'We don't want to go back to the villages,' I said aggressively. 'We just want to go home.'

'You won't have to go back,' he said calmly.

'What, never?' I couldn't believe I was hearing him right.

He smiled. 'You will never have to go back to the villages, you have my word.'

For a moment I couldn't get my breath. 'Why?' I couldn't believe my ears.

'Because you don't have to go back there any more,' he shrugged. 'You can live here in Taiz for a while.'

I didn't trust him at first. It was like a dream come true. Slowly, from the low point of being in Campais, life was getting better and my struggles were beginning to pay off. First I had got back to Hockail and close to Nadia, now I had got to Taiz with her and out of the village. The next stop must be to get back home to England.

What we didn't know was that elsewhere in the City the National Security Police were picking up and interrogating everyone who had had anything to do with Eileen and Ben – the hospital director, the interpreter and the driver. They were all having to write statements, and were being questioned to see if any of them had had any idea that the English woman was a journalist. None of them had known anything, of course, or they would never have dared to help them.

Nadia and I both grew to like Abdul Walli during that time because he seemed to talk to us straight. He was fatherly towards us, and always told us how he felt and what he thought was going on. He didn't seem to be hiding anything from us, and I didn't hide anything from him. Although he understood what I was saying, I don't think he really understood how we felt about going

169

home. I don't think anybody out there understood how strongly we felt, how much we hated the life in the villages and how determined we were to escape. The best feeling was that with him looking after us we were safe from Abdul Khada and the others. No-one could do anything to us as long as Abdul Walli was in charge. At least as far as we were concerned he was in charge, although I knew that he was only doing as the Government told him, and wasn't in a position to make the ultimate decisions about our fate himself.

When he told us that we just needed to sign papers and then we could have our children back, we went along with it. The letters were addressed 'to whom it may concern', and in them we publicly accepted that we were married to our husbands and happy with them, that we were now living in Taiz and all our problems were over. Abdul Walli gave us the text to copy in our own handwriting and then asked us to sign them, saying that if we did that we would have our children back by the end of the week. We did as he suggested because we trusted him more than anyone else and because we wanted the kids.

We had to stay inside the house during these days, although we were allowed to wander from room to room and up onto the roof to get some fresh air. The most important thing for us was being together. We didn't mind being prisoners as long as we had each other. There was a massive modern kitchen on the roof, complete with fridge, sink, washing machine and liquidiser, things we hadn't seen since we left England.

There were several commanders in Taiz like Abdul Walli, each with little police forces of their own. The policemen were inside the walls of the compound with us, but they sat in a building which was across the yard from the house. All the men had handguns, and some of them carried rifles over their shoulders as well. As we watched them strolling around the grounds from the roof, and sitting idly in groups talking, we felt very free and very safe at the same time.

On the fourth day we were sitting in the house, talking, when Abdul Walli came in unexpectedly. 'Here are your children,' he said, and we could hardly believe our eyes. They had been brought down from the villages with Abdul Noor and Shiab, Gowad's eldest son. Shiab and his sister were going back to stay with their grandparents, but Marcus, Haney and Tina were staying with us. We were so relieved. Marcus was just starting to walk and I swept him up into my arms. They told me that ever since I had gone he had done nothing but cry for me.

CHAPTER SIXTEEN

Living In The City

A few days later Abdullah and Mohammed, our so-called 'husbands' arrived in the city from Saudi Arabia. They had been ordered by the Government to come and sort the situation out. Abdul Walli had warned us they were coming but hadn't told us when. We were in the women's sitting room when he came in to see us.

'Your husbands are in the next room,' he told us. 'Do you want to come out and say hello to them?'

We reluctantly did as he asked. They were sitting waiting for us, both looking worried by what was happening. We sat down and talked politely for a few moments, then Abdul Walli left the room. Mohammed had grown enormously fat, but Abdullah was as skinny as ever.

'What's going on?' Mohammed wanted to know. 'We hear all these rumours but we don't know what is happening. We have heard about newspaper stories in England and we have heard rumours that your mother is coming out. What's happening?'

I felt safe and didn't have to hide anything any more. I felt confident that Abdul Walli wouldn't let us be taken back to the villages now, so I told him.

'Mum's doing everything she can to get us out of here. What you and your Dads have done to us is wrong, and we are never going to accept it. That's the way it has to be.'

172

Abdullah remained silent.

When Abdul Walli returned, the boys asked to be allowed to use the telephone. He agreed and they called Gowad in England and Abdul Khada in Saudi. Both fathers told their sons that they must not divorce us, and they must not let us have the children. They didn't want us back in England causing them embarrassment, and they didn't believe we would leave the kids. Their fathers told them that they should agree to stay in Taiz, as long as their wives and children stayed with them. Arab men never disobey their fathers, so they refused to consider any alternative. We had reached another barrier to our escape.

We couldn't all stay at the house now; there were too many of us. So Abdul Walli found us a flat which was about a five minute taxi ride away, and all four of us moved into it with the three children. I didn't care where I went at that stage, as long as I was with Nadia and the kids and as long as I didn't have to go back to Hockail. I felt that as long as I was in Taiz, and had connections with Abdul Walli, I could keep up my campaign for getting home to England.

The flat was in a rough area, in a three-storey block down a narrow, broken-down street. We were on the second floor. There was a massive hallway in the flat with two bedrooms and a living room leading off it, a bathroom and kitchen. There was a balcony overlooking the street below.

We knew that we were going to have to sleep with Mohammed and Abdullah, there was not going to be any option. Even though we were in the city we knew what the rules and regulations were about marriage. I knew that the whole ordeal was nearly over, so I didn't want to cause unnecessary trouble between us. Marcus slept in the same room as Abdullah and me and Nadia's kids slept with her and Mohammed.

They had brought our mattresses from the villages, which we laid on the cold stone floors, but there was no

173

other furniture in the flat except for a television which ran off the electricity. I still had my tape recorder. In the kitchen there was a sink and small gas stove and a shelf. There was a shower in the bathroom but no hot water. We had all we needed, and I was just happy to be with Nadia all day. Although it was a slum compared to anywhere I had lived in England, it was a dream come true when compared to living in the villages of Mokbana. It was so wonderful not to have to work from morning to night, to be able to stay in bed until the afternoons if we felt like it.

The boys behaved just as normal. They were out of the flat most of the day with friends in the city, and we never bothered to ask where they went; we weren't interested. As long as we had each other we preferred to be left alone.

Abdullah's brother, Mohammed, and Bakela were still living in Taiz and used to come to visit us from time to time. Now that the Government was involved no-one spoke any more about our situation. We did not discuss the past, we were all just waiting to see what happened next. Nadia and I were quite happy to cut the past out of our minds.

To start with Nadia and I didn't go out much. We felt strangely scared of the bustling streets, the cars and all the men wandering around. After seven years of virtual captivity in the villages we found the prospect of freedom overpowering. Even when we went out onto the balcony to hang our washing up to dry we would veil ourselves in case there was anyone watching from any of the other windows. We had become just like the village women we had been living amongst, modest and frightened of the open world because we had forgotten how to deal with it. The boys would bring the food back to us and anything else we needed to survive, while we stayed indoors.

Sometimes the boys would go up to Abdul Walli's house in the afternoon to chew *qat*, and we would go up

174

with them for the ride and to sit talking with the other women visiting the house. Abdul Walli never came down to the flat to visit us. We always had the children with us and they seemed to be quite happy as long as we were around. But if either Nadia or I left the room they would start crying and running after us. I guess they were frightened we would leave them again. Haney was the worst, always clinging to Nadia if she went anywhere, crying and asking her where she was going. When we were all there they played well together.

In England Mum was running into as many frustrations as we were in Taiz. Alf Dickens had got her involved with the *Daily Mail*, and she was beginning to realise that she was just being used to get them an exclusive story and to cut Eileen and the *Observer* out. She went back to Eileen and was spending Christmas Day with her and her family at her London home, dazed and confused by all the different advice and the demands which were being made on her.

The Yemeni Ambassador in London had issued a statement, saying that he now understood that Nadia and I had met and married our husbands in Birmingham, and had then gone to live in the Yemen. Problems had only arisen, according to him, when Mum left Dad.

This was Dad's latest story, and contradicted everything he had said to journalists so far, when he had admitted that we had gone on holiday and then met the boys we were secretly married to. The Ambassador also said that if Mum wanted to visit the Yemen and sort out the family problems, she would be given every assistance by the Yemeni Government to bring her daughters home.

In Taiz our lives continued as if none of this was going on. We began to go out visiting other people's houses to pass the time. We began to meet some very different women to the ones we had grown used to in the villages. The wives who came to the city with their husbands were

175

more modern in their outlook and they used to like to go around to one another's houses for visits. Unlike the village women they didn't have to work all day fetching water and grinding corn, they had time on their hands. They would travel, usually veiled, in taxis from one house to another, visiting friends and relatives. Because so few people had ever come to visit Ward and me it took me a while to get used to this social life.

A lot of them obviously wanted to find out what was happening to us but they must have been warned that I was very aggressive when people asked me questions, so they usually kept quiet about it. The odd one would ask me if we were going home or if Mum was coming for us, and I would just tell them to mind their own business. Most of them were all right. Our health was beginning to improve and I began to feel much better in myself, less tired and depressed.

I always had the telephone in Abdul Walli's room on my mind, but I never had the guts to ask if I could use it to call Mum. One day someone high up must have told Abdul Walli to let us phone home. They wanted us to tell her what was happening and what a change for the better there had been in our lives since leaving the villages. They hoped we would tell her how great it was and that she could stop making a fuss and stop talking to the papers now. No way. The closer I got to leaving, the sooner I wanted to leave.

We were telling Abdul Walli and the others that we were feeling better and happier, and playing them at their own game. We were lying to them just like they were lying to us, not so much by what they said, but by what they didn't say and by what they didn't do. They were hoping that they wouldn't have to do any more for us, that the whole thing would just quieten down now that we were away from Mokbana. We were willing to let them think that that was what was happening, but we weren't going to tell Mum to stop working on getting us out.

176

Ashia answered the phone and couldn't believe that it was actually me speaking, she asked me all sorts of questions about my past to check that it really was me. Then she fetched Mum. We talked for a while and she told us that she was going to come out to Taiz to see us again.

A few weeks later we were told that we were going to receive a phone call from England, and we went to Abdul Walli's house to take it. It was Mum, ringing to see how we were, and telling us not to worry because things were happening and she was still coming to see us. I did all the talking because Nadia was too shy.

'I've got a friend here who wants to say hello to you,' she said.

'Oh yeah.' I was surprised but I didn't say anything, I was willing to go along with anything she wanted.

'His name's Tom.'

'OK.' I was puzzled, and then Tom Quirke came on the line. I didn't know who he was at that stage, but later I discovered that he was the local reporter who had started the story and that he was talking to me on the radio, broadcasting the conversation all over the Birmingham area. They couldn't tell me that was what they were doing in case the lines were cut at our end. Anyone can listen in to a telephone conversation out there.

'How are you, Zana?' he asked.

'OK.' I was guarded because I didn't know who he was.

'Do you still want to come home to Birmingham, Zana?' he asked.

'Yes,' I answered, 'I still want to come home, as quickly as possible.'

'What do you miss most about home?'

'My friends.' After a few more questions he handed me back to Mum.

Then we received a call from Dad. He was on the phone for over an hour, begging us not to come home because he would die of shame. He kept saying, 'If you love me, don't come home.' Well, we didn't love him and he must have known that. He begged us to stay in Taiz until the press had forgotten about the story. I told him he would be lucky. He said he would kill himself if we came home and I said 'Good'.

All the time we were in Taiz we heard rumours that more stories were appearing in the papers and the problem was getting bigger and bigger for the Government. Abdul Walli seemed to be getting more and more concerned. I guess he was being given a hard time by his superiors, who wanted to know why he wasn't able to calm the situation down.

Whenever we talked about the foreign media coverage and he tried to persuade us that we should accept things now and tell Mum to stop her campaign, I would just say, 'But it's the truth what they are writing in the papers', and he couldn't say any more.

At one stage he showed me our marriage certificates. They were written in Arabic but I could read enough to understand what they said. He showed them to me to prove that they were genuine.

'It's false as far as I'm concerned,' I told him angrily. 'I have studied the Koran and I know it says it is wrong to force a girl into marriage, so I don't accept that those certificates are genuine.'

Although we knew that he was only acting on orders, Nadia and I both looked on Abdul Walli as our saviour as he was the one who had actually got us out of the villages. He was the first man we had met who had treated us well and we loved him for that. As well as the wife he had in the city, he had another in his own village. I was told she had about six children by him, as well as the child which the wife in Taiz had. I don't know whether they are allowed to have more than one wife, but it seemed to me that the rich men in the Yemen can do what they please.

Slowly Nadia and I got used to being back in the real

world. We started by going out in taxis with the children, just riding around town. The cars would pick us up from the front door and drop us back there, so we didn't have to walk anywhere.

After a while we felt brave enough to stop the cars and get out and do some shopping, buying food or clothes for the kids, but always wearing our veils and traditional clothes. We wanted to get to know the city a bit because by then we realised we were going to be stuck there for a while, so we might as well make the most of it. It was a difficult city to like, dirty and overcrowded, but we were always happy if we were together, and we began to feel more like the free English girls we had once been.

The violence of life out there, even in the city, was illustrated by the public executions held in the town squares, where crowds of people would gather, including women and children, to watch prisoners being machine-gunned to death.

Being veiled made us invisible. No-one knew who we were and we felt able to disappear in the crowd. That felt wonderful after being watched and talked about every moment of the day for all those years.

One day we were at Abdul Walli's house when three important looking women came to see us. They were very different from the women we were used to. They looked as if they had jobs and money. They looked healthy and wore jewellery. They carried books and pens and papers. One of them worked for the Governor of Taiz as his secretary, the other two were something to do with a women's association which had been set up in the city. They had heard about us and wanted to know more about our story. The secretary said she had been sent by the Governor to find out more about us.

'You can go and tell the Governor it is none of his business,' I snapped, in my usual manner.

'There is no need to talk like that,' she said firmly. 'We have come to see you as friends. We aren't going to do anything with the information you give us, we just want to hear how you lived and what happened to you, so that perhaps we can help other girls like you.'

I realised that she meant it and so Nadia and I told them all about life in the villages, and the work which we had to do. They were obviously shocked. Even though they were Yemeni women they had never imagined that such things went on in their own country. They thought that planting and grinding the corn by hand was something that their ancestors did, they had no idea that some people were still living like that. We told them again how unhappy we were and that we just wanted to go home. They tried to explain to us that we were Yemeni citizens now.

'I know what I am,' I said stubbornly, 'and I know what I want. I want to go home.' I felt that I was like a dripping tap, steadily going on and on until I had finally worn them down and made them accept that they weren't going to be able to persuade me to change my mind and stay.

The three women must have been briefed by the same people as Abdul Walli because they came up with all the same arguments about staying in the city, and I gave them the same answers I had given him. I could see they weren't satisfied by what I had said, but they said goodbye politely and left.

A few days later we heard that Mum was on her way. She was flying down from Sana'a with Jim Halley, the British Consul, and an official from the Ministry of Foreign Affairs who could help them with translations. At last, we thought, something else is going to happen; but nothing was going smoothly for Mum.

To get a visa for the Yemen, she had had to travel to the Yemeni Embassy in London. She went with Eileen and Ben. When they got there in a taxi they found the building surrounded with film crews, photographers and reporters. Mum flattened herself on the taxi floor and they drove on to a pub round the corner. The Embassy officials were then phoned and asked to bring the papers to her there. They came to see Mum and took away her passport and application and said they would be back in half an hour. They told Mum to wait for them.

When the papers were finally all in order she was whisked through Gatwick Airport like a VIP and flown to Sana'a with a member of the Lufthansa flight crew looking after her at all times.

Jim met her in Sana'a and took her to a small hotel near his house, and the next day they went to the Ministry of Foreign Affairs, who had insisted on seeing Mum before she could travel to Taiz. Everyone claimed to be too busy to see them when they got there, and told them that they were not to contact us by phone. Jim went back later and met another contact of his who arranged for them to fly to Taiz. The airport, however, was fog-bound, and no flights took off until the following afternoon.

Finally, however, they were in the air and on their way to us.

CHAPTER SEVENTEEN

Red Tape And Official Persecution

We were told that there was going to be a big meeting in the Governor's building. Mum, the British Consul and the Yemeni official were going to be there, and we were told to attend with Mohammed and Abdullah, and the children.

We went up to Abdul Walli's house to wait for Mum to get in on the plane from Sana'a. When she arrived he went outside to greet her while we waited in the women's sitting room. He brought her in. She was carrying a single suitcase. We greeted her quite calmly, emotions weren't running as high as before, perhaps because we felt we were nearer to getting away, perhaps because we were growing too hard to let our feelings show any more. Nadia cried but I didn't.

It was the first time Mum had seen the little kids. She seemed surprised by the luxury that Abdul Walli lived in. When she sat down she let out an exclamation, 'Gosh! What comfortable chairs.' She made me laugh. It must have been a big surprise to her if she was expecting to find a house like the one in Hockail.

Abdul Walli and his wife were in the room, as were Abdullah and Mohammed. She avoided looking at the two boys. It was obvious how she felt about them: she thought they were beneath contempt. Abdul Walli made polite conversation for a few minutes and then he took

182

the boys out to the hut where they all used to sit talking and chewing.

Mum was left alone with Nadia, me and the kids. We were able to tell her everything that had happened since we last met, while she told us what was happening at her end. She had brought the kids some toys from England. There was a doll for Tina, a lorry with cars on it for Haney and a merry-go-round for Marcus. They were all over the moon with the presents, and started to play while we talked.

Mum was exhausted, but she looked much better than the last time. She told us about Jim and about everything that had happened to them in Sana'a, and about the meeting we were all going to have to go to.

It was due to happen the following day, so we took her back to the flat to sleep. She came in with me and Nadia and the children. There was a single bed for her and the rest of us slept on the floor on mattresses. The boys had to sleep alone, Mohammed in his room and Abdullah in the sitting room. There was no way that Mum would accept that we had to sleep with them. She told us we had to stop with her now she was there. I knew that if anyone found out about that we would get into trouble, but there was no arguing with her. The only thing that worried me was that Abdul Khada might hear what was going on and come from Saudi Arabia to make more trouble for us. I was still frightened of him, even now that we were in the city. I was pretty sure he wouldn't come because he was scared by the way things were getting out of his control, but he was always a haunting presence at the back of my thoughts.

The next morning we had breakfast and prepared ourselves for the meeting. Nadia and I started to get dressed in all the black clothes and veils, and Mum was complaining. She couldn't understand why we still had to dress like that now that we were out of the villages. She didn't like the idea of us covering our faces. 'You're free now, you're British,' she said. 'Dress as you want.' But

183

we couldn't do it, we were still scared and we clung onto the clothes which allowed us to hide from the world. Neither of us felt strong enough to face such important men in disrespectful clothing. It would have made us feel naked. I was very aware that we still weren't free, and I didn't want to antagonise them now and risk them throwing Mum out of the country, or shipping us back to the villages.

Jim came to meet us at the flat before we left. He seemed a very pleasant man, very tall with short, gingery hair and a Scottish accent.

The taxi arrived and took us to the Governor's massive building, about four storeys high and full of offices. We climbed two flights of stairs and came into a big lounge with a desk at one end, and black leather settees and chairs all around. We sat down to wait and the room slowly began to fill up with men. The official from the Ministry was there with the Governor and three male secretaries. Abdullah and Mohammed were also there.

The official was doing most of the talking. He seemed very educated, with a good English accent. He wanted to hear our story, so we told the whole thing over again.

Marcus was playing up and he wouldn't stop crying. He wanted to run around and make a noise. At one point the Governor became angry and told me to shut him up. Anyone with small children knows that there is nothing you can do when they are like that, so I just ignored him and eventually Marcus calmed down enough for me to tell the story. Haney was sitting on Nadia's lap listening to what was going on with big, wide eyes, and Tina was asleep.

As I talked, all the men in the room were silent. I looked round at them and they all had their heads bowed, as if they were ashamed of what had happened and of the way we had been treated. I told them about not knowing we were married when we came to the Yemen and of being forced to sleep with the boys. I wasn't being aggressive, I was just telling the story straight without sounding angry. Nadia answered some questions as well.

'Are you happy now?' The Home Secretary asked eventually.

'No.' I spoke firmly.

He nodded and started to tell us their rules governing what had to happen in a situation like this.

'If you left the Yemen,' he said, 'you would have to leave the children here, you know that.'

'Why?' I interrupted. 'They are our children. They are illegitimate anyway, they don't belong to their fathers because we aren't married to them, so why can't we keep them?'

He didn't like it when I answered back, none of the men did, but I had to speak up for myself. They tried to stop me talking, but I wouldn't. Jim didn't try to stop me, he didn't want me to stop now that we had got this far.

'How would it be if we got visas for all of you,' the official asked, 'and you all travelled together? Would you go with your husbands to England? Otherwise there is no way you will be able to leave this country with your children. If you go with the men you will be able to take the children.'

Nadia and I looked at each other. 'OK,' we said. We would have said anything to get out of the Yemen with the kids.

'And what about you two,' he turned to the boys, 'would you be willing to travel to England with your wives and children if we can arrange it?' The boys both nodded their agreement to the plan.

'All right then.' He seemed relieved to have found a possible solution. 'We will organise visas for Mohammed and Abdullah.'

That seemed to be the end of the meeting. Everything would now depend on the British Home Office agreeing to give visas to the boys. That meant we had to go back to waiting while they were contacted and made up their minds. Jim said he thought they would say no, because they would think the whole thing was a plot to get the boys into Britain, since they all knew that Nadia and I had often said how much we hated the boys. But he agreed that if that was the only way to get the children to England it would have to happen somehow.

Jim had some application forms for them to fill in, so we all went off to a smaller room. The boys had to prove they could support themselves in England, and Mohammed told Jim he had £12,000 saved from working in Saudi Arabia. Later we discovered that both Mohammed and Abdullah lied to Jim that day. In fact Mohammed had no money at all, and Abdullah told him he had never over-stayed a visa in Britain before, which he had done while undergoing medical treatment. At that stage Jim thought they were telling the truth and he told us that normally the British Home Office would take six months to respond to applications like these, but he promised he would try to hurry them along.

While Mum was in the Yemen she discovered that Abdul Khada and Gowad had sent application forms to the British Embassy in Sana'a in 1980, on behalf of their sons, asking that they should be allowed to come to Britain on the basis that they were married to British nationals. They received a letter from the Vice Consul telling them that their wives would have to accompany them to the Embassy for an interview. Knowing that they couldn't do that, because of the way they had tricked us into illegal marriages, they did not pursue the matter. The British Embassy in Sana'a, however, still have those application forms, demonstrating that one of the main reasons why we were 'bought' from Dad was for our British citizenship.

Mum stayed with us in the flat for four weeks. The boys stayed out of her way most of the time, so it was just Mum, Nadia, me, and the kids, together, which was great. When the boys were around there were occasional fights, with them threatening to tell the Governor to send Mum home because she was interfering with their marital lives.

Everyone heard different rumours at that time. Someone said that Gowad and Abdul Khada had bribed the Governor. Someone else said we would be leaving in six months, while another person said they had heard we would never leave. Someone rang and told us they could get us out in a week because they knew the President, while someone else said that Dad had written a letter to the Government which would ensure that we were never allowed to go. But nothing actually happened.

One day Mum decided to fly down to Sana'a to collect money and her passport, which Jim had taken to get her visa extended. She suggested we went with her for the day out. When we got to Taiz airport to catch the internal flight, we found our pictures had been stuck up on a board and the guards had been told that we were trying to flee the country. We were taken straight back to Abdul Walli's house.

The three women who had talked to us previously at Abdul Walli's came to see Mum at the flat. They left us their addresses and said that we were welcome to go and visit them if Mum got bored and wanted something to do. Mum did get bored in the flat so we took them up on their offer. They had nice houses, like smaller versions of Abdul Walli's. They all provided lovely food and lived quite westernised lives, with western clothes and uncovered heads. They could read and write, they had been to college and had travelled.

One of the women from the Women's Association was particularly nice and understanding. I got talking to her about the cut which Nadia was given by the old woman when she gave birth to Tina. Nadia was still getting an occasional discharge from it, and the woman seemed very concerned about it. She told me to bring Nadia over and she would arrange a taxi to take us to see a woman

187

doctor friend of hers. We never told Mum about it because we didn't want to worry her.

The doctor's surgery was in a nice area of the city. It was like a family planning clinic. We went straight in. She gave me a check-up first, then she did the same thing to Nadia. She immediately knew that Nadia had an infection. She gave her some tablets for it. She asked us if we were using any form of contraception and she was shocked when we said 'no'. We were constantly frightened of getting pregnant. The only precaution we could take was trying to avoid having sex as much as possible. It was just luck that we had only become pregnant as few times as we had. The doctor was horrified to hear that, and gave us both supplies of the pill. Mum was delighted, and reminded us every night to take them.

My brother Ahmed also came to visit us while Mum was there, which was the first time she had seen him since he was three. We were all in the flat when he knocked on the door. Mum had no idea who he was, she just stood looking at him like a stranger. I had to introduce them and then they hugged. They couldn't talk directly to one another because of the language-barrier so they had to talk through us. Dad's brother was with him, having arrived in the Yemen from Saudi Arabia. He said that he was on our side and against everything that Dad had done to us. He was ashamed of all the publicity. He was a nice man. He looked exactly like Dad although he was a few years younger.

Meeting Ahmed made Mum very happy, she was all smiles after that. He wanted to know if she could help him get out of the Yemen as well, he had had enough of the army by then. He was depressed and he wanted to come to England. She said she would organise it. Mum phoned Jim and he told her to send Ahmed to the British Embassy and that there would be a passport waiting for him once he had filled in the relevant forms. There was no problem because Ahmed was a British subject. Dad found out what was happening and did everything he could to stop it. I suppose he was ashamed of all the things he had done and didn't want to have to face up to Ahmed.

My uncle and Ahmed were staying with relatives in Taiz whom we knew nothing about, and took us to visit them. They were a nice family who had left their village a long time ago to move to the city. Their elder son was a doctor and they were quite westernised. The woman was Dad's cousin and she told me a bit about Dad before he left Aden. She told me he was married in Marais as a boy, which was the first time Mum or I had heard any details about it. She told us that after he left for England he wrote to his young wife telling her he would never come back and the story was that she died of a broken heart.

One morning my uncle came to see us and asked if we knew where Ahmed was. They were both still staying with the relatives we had met, but my brother had disappeared. None of us could imagine where he was so we all took a trip up to Abdul Walli's house in a taxi to see if he could find out what had happened. Uncle went in to talk to Abdul Walli, who said he didn't know anything about it, but promised to look into it. He got some of his contacts to look around and they came back to say Ahmed was in prison.

I didn't wait for Abdul Walli to do anything about it. I got into a taxi with Mum, Uncle, Nadia and the kids and went down to the main prison where they said he was. There was a uniformed guard outside the big steel gate. He was holding a rifle, and I asked if Ahmed Muhsen was inside. The guard was quite friendly. I suppose he was surprised to be talked to by a veiled woman in the street, but he didn't show it. He said he would go in and find out. A few minutes later he came out and said Ahmed was in there.

'Why has he been locked up?' I demanded to know, but he couldn't tell me. 'I want to see him,' I persisted.

189

'No,' he shook his head, 'you're not allowed to. He's on his way now to see the main warden and then he will be released.'

'Have you been paid to say that?' I shouted. 'Everything runs by money, all of you only do anything if someone pays you.'

He lifted his rifle and pointed it at me. 'If you don't shut your mouth … ' he snarled, and then went quiet.

'Go on,' I said, 'you do it.' My uncle grabbed my arm and tried to pull me away.

'Cool down Zana,' he warned, and I realised there was no point shouting at a prison guard. We all got back into the taxi and drove back to the flat.

Later in the day one of Abdul Walli's policemen came to the flat and said that they had found out more about what had happened. Ahmed had been jailed because he and Uncle had been plotting to kidnap us and get us out of the country. Ahmed had been called to see the Governor of Taiz. When he got to the office they had arrested him. It was the first we had heard of any such plot.

Nadia and I decided to go and see the Governor ourselves, leaving Mum back at the flat with Uncle. When we got to the official building we barged our way through the security people and on the way up the stairs we bumped into the secretary who had come to visit us before. She invited us into her little office. I was so angry I didn't care what I said. She tried to calm me down by phoning through to the Governor to tell him we were there. We were brought tea and then left in the little room.

We never got in to see the Governor. They contacted Abdul Walli instead and he had to come and fetch us. He was furious with us for acting on our own but I told him I didn't care. 'Come home now,' he ordered us.

'I'm not going anywhere,' I said, 'until they let my brother go.'

'Come on then,' he said, 'we'll go and get him.'

190

We went out to a taxi and drove down to the prison again. Abdul Walli went in to talk to the officials, while we waited in the taxi outside. It was about half an hour before he came out again. He had Ahmed with him.

Ahmed climbed into the taxi and as we drove back to the flat he told us that he had been beaten up by a guard while he was inside. They had warned him to stop interfering in our case, that it was a family matter which had nothing to do with him. I felt sorry for him because he didn't do any harm. They were just assuming he was plotting; they had no proof of anything. But the officials over there don't need proof before they act against someone. When we got back to the flat Mum was very relieved to see Ahmed again.

One day when Mum and Nadia and I were alone in the flat with the kids, there was a knock on the door. I answered it and found a policeman, dressed in the usual paramilitary uniform, complete with beret and rifle, standing there with an official looking man in a long white gown.

'Is your mother in?' the official asked angrily.

'Yes, through there.' I pointed to the sitting room, where Mum and Nadia were sitting on the mattresses which we had spread around the bare room instead of furniture. They marched through and the official began shouting at Mum in broken English.

'Miriam Ali,' he said, 'I tell you that your visa to visit the Yemen has run out. You are breaking the law by being here.'

'No it hasn't.' Mum refused to be intimidated. 'It's still got four more days to run.'

'Do you know what would happen to you if you went over the closing date?' he asked, threateningly, as the policeman fingered his rifle trigger.

'But it hasn't run out,' Mum repeated.

'Let me see your passport,' he ordered.

Mum handed him her passport and he began thumbing through it. 'Who told you to come here to see me?' she asked, but he wouldn't answer. 'Give me back my passport,' she shouted, 'and get out of this house. Don't bother me again, I've still got four days to go and I'm not leaving until my time is up.' She was shaking with anger that they should try to scare her off in such a crude manner. The men left, still making threatening noises.

Just as Jim had expected, the British Home Office turned down the request for visas. They had discovered that the boys had lied on their application forms and so they were not to be allowed into Britain. Then I knew that there was no way we were going to be able to get out of the Yemen with our children. I knew I was going to have to leave Marcus behind, and I could hardly bear to think about it. There was no point in Mum staying any longer, she decided that it would be better for her to go back to England and continue the fight from there. There was nothing else to do in Taiz at that stage.

Nadia and I took the kids with us in Abdul Walli's Land Rover to see her off from Taiz airport. It is a new, glass building, and you can see the planes on the tarmac from the other side. We only had to wait about ten minutes before Mum's plane arrived. It is hard to describe the horrible feeling of watching her leave again, when all we wanted to do was get on the plane with her. Nadia, Mum and I were all crying. Seeing Nadia crying started Haney off as well.

'Not to worry,' she told us, 'it's nearly over now.'

Abdul Walli was allowed to walk through the customs with her, and we stood waving from the other side of the windows. He stood on the tarmac watching until she was safely on board and then came back into the building to join us. We waited to watch the plane take off before driving back to town. We all stayed silent on the way back, and Abdul Walli knew better than to try to talk to us.

On the road out to the airport they had built a big, new park with a funfair for the children. Mohammed and Abdullah came with us one time for a day out with the kids. The kids had a good time that day.

Mohammed and Abdullah were more like brothers to the kids than fathers. I never saw Abdullah showing any affection towards Marcus at all. If ever I needed new clothes for the boy I always had to ask, he would never volunteer to buy him anything.

My uncle and Ahmed stayed on in Taiz for a while after Mum left. One day my uncle took me aside. 'Listen Zana,' he said, 'look at all the trouble you are getting into here. Why don't you come back to Marais with us, we can arrange everything for you through Aden.'

'What do we want to go to Marais for?' I asked. 'What could we do there?'

'We could do a lot there. Our Government is completely different to the Yemen. They can't interfere with us.'

I thought about it seriously, but I decided I didn't want to take the risk. We had got this far and although I thought I trusted my uncle, it was just possible that Dad had persuaded him to arrange this, and we would get to Marais and find we were right back where we started. I knew that Dad and Abdul Khada were capable of doing that.

Somehow Abdul Walli found out about my uncle's idea. 'I hear your uncle is taking you to Marais,' he said to me one day, and I couldn't understand how the rumours had got to him. With Mum gone Nadia and I started to feel insecure again, even though we were in the city. We didn't know what was going on and it was all very confusing. We carried on visiting the same people and living with Mohammed and Abdullah, who had to keep looking after us all.

One day Marcus became very sick again. He was not eating and becoming very thin, and had grown too weak to do anything, whereas before he had been hyperactive. This time Nadia and I took him to the hospital ourselves.

193

News of the meeting at the Governor's house had spread through the city. The Governor's building had been full of people that day, and our story was now well known. We found that even if we wore veils people still recognised us in the street if we were with the kids, or if they overheard us talking in English. When we got to the hospital somebody must have recognised us and no-one tried to stop us as we stormed through the waiting room.

We walked straight into a doctor's office and I demanded that someone look at my child. I was told to hold on a minute and another man was called to see us. I didn't know if he was a doctor or what he was, but he obviously knew who we were and he spoke to us very kindly. I didn't care who he was as long as someone was looking at Marcus. He told us to follow him and led us into a room which was equipped like a laboratory, with people doing X-rays and blood tests and things.

'Sit down,' he told us, 'let's look at the young man.' He took a look at Marcus for a few minutes. 'He's very weak. I think we should do some blood tests,' he said eventually. He took some samples of blood from him.

'How long will it take before we know?' I asked.

'Come back tomorrow,' he said. 'Come straight to this part of the building and I'll be here.'

The next day we went back as we had been told and the doctor was there. He looked very serious when we went in.

'Have you got the results?' I asked.

'Yes,' he nodded, 'Marcus needs blood very badly. He is very close to dying. He's a lucky child. If you hadn't got him here I don't think he would have lived much longer.'

'Where am I going to get the blood from?' I asked.

'It will have to come from the father.'

'I don't want him to have anything from his father,' I said quickly, imagining all the pints of strange blood which Abdullah had had pumped into him in Saudi Arabia during his operation. 'I don't want Marcus to have anything from him.'

194

'All right.' The doctor seemed to understand. 'I'll give him some of mine then, if my group matches his.' He tested himself and his group matched. He called another doctor over and asked him to take a bagful of blood from him. It was wonderful how he seemed to feel he was part of it with us, and that he had to help in some way. I don't know why he acted like that, perhaps he felt sorry about what had happened to us and wanted to make up for it in some way. Once they had the blood they laid Marcus down on the table. He was so weak that day that he could hardly open his eyes.

'What are you going to do?' I asked.

'We have to find one of his veins and then we will pump the blood in slowly,' the doctor explained.

They were searching along his arm but they couldn't find a vein and I started to panic. He had a very distinct vein running across his forehead and they decided they would have to use that. I started to cry.

As they pushed the needle into his forehead he screamed and struggled. I picked him up and held him, watching the blood pumping into my baby's head. I had to stay completely still in case the needle became dislodged. It seemed to flow so slowly and after a moment Marcus fell asleep. The blood kept on pumping for two hours. It was the most horrible feeling imaginable, watching this happening to my baby, and knowing that soon I was going to be leaving him. I was petrified that something was going to go wrong. Nadia was with me, but no-one else knew where we were or what was happening.

I told Nadia to go and find someone and tell them where we were and arrange some transport for us when we finished. She went back to the flat but neither of the boys was there. She found a taxi and went up to Abdul Walli's house and fetched him. By the time they got back to the hospital Abdul Walli looked scared and wanted to know what was happening. I guess they would have held him responsible if anything had happened to Marcus while we were in his care.

The doctor came back every so often to check that I was all right. Abdul Walli thanked him for everything that he had done. As the blood finished pumping Marcus's colour had changed from yellow to red, and we took him back to the flat. The blood seemed to have been all he needed, and within a few days he was starting to eat and looking better. It seemed that he was always going to have health problems like his father.

One of the reasons that I was able to contemplate leaving him in the Yemen was because he was a boy, and I knew that he would be all right. If I had had a girl I don't know what I would have done. But it would have been easier to leave a fit and strong boy than one who found living such a struggle.

CHAPTER EIGHTEEN

An Abrupt Parting

Jim telephoned us at Abdul Walli's after Mum left, and asked to speak to Mohammed. He told him that he was entitled to a British passport because Gowad, his father, now had British nationality.

'Can you come to Sana'a to sort out the paperwork?' Jim asked.

'Yes, all right,' Mohammed agreed. He seemed pleased at the prospect.

To me this sounded like good news. It looked like a good chance to get Nadia and her kids out of the country first, which was what I wanted if it wasn't possible for us all to travel together. I didn't want her to be left behind on her own because I didn't think she would have the strength or the will to keep up the fight without me.

Although he was keen to go to Britain, Mohammed didn't seem to be in a hurry to go down to Sana'a to see Jim. Nadia and I kept on at him all the time to do it, and eventually he asked if we all wanted to go with him. Abdul Walli told me that my passport was also ready with Jim in Sana'a, and I needed to collect it. Mum had left our papers with Jim because she didn't trust us to hold onto them ourselves. She thought if we had them it would be too easy for the men to get them off us, and they would disappear the same way as the originals.

Nadia and I, and the kids, set out for Sana'a with Abdul Walli and one of his policemen in the Land

197

Rover. Although Mohammed was coming with us to collect his passport, Abdullah didn't come. I didn't know where he was, but it didn't bother me. As usual we set out early in the morning for the four hour drive.

Abdul Walli had a house on the outskirts of Sana'a where we were all going to stay while we did our business there. It was another nice house, although a bit smaller than the one in Taiz. The weather was very cold and wet, and the house seemed deserted after the bustle of the Taiz police station. All the neighbouring homes were owned by other rich people and were surrounded by high walls. There are dramatic contrasts between the rich and poor areas in both cities.

Abdul Walli told us that the house next door was owned by a solicitor, and there was a doctor living opposite. They were both much richer and grander houses than his. An English oilman and his family lived in one of the other houses nearby. As soon as we arrived at the house the men went out to buy food for us, bringing it back for Nadia and me to cook.

When Mohammed went to the Embassy for his passport there was some sort of technical problem. They told him that they still needed Gowad to fill in a form, which he was refusing to do. His father obviously didn't want him to come to England if it meant Nadia coming too. Mohammed, like Abdullah, always did what his father told him, and wouldn't hear of any criticism of Gowad, but I was sure that Gowad was deliberately holding things up. Nadia wanted to be on his passport as well as her own, to make sure the kids could travel with her.

Nadia collected my passport from Jim when she went in to see him with Mohammed. I waited outside in the Land Rover and she gave it to me as soon as she came out. It was the first time I had seen a British passport because Dad and Abdul Khada had always kept hold of my first one. As soon as I got it, however, I had to give it to Abdul Walli. He told me he had to get some official stamps in it from the Yemen Home Office.

We took a drive round the city that day. It was a nice city, big and full of old buildings. It was a lot more westernised than Taiz, more like I remembered English cities being. There were women walking around in western clothes, some of them holding hands with their husbands. There were tourists on the streets and everything looked a lot cleaner.

All the children started to catch colds from the winds on the second day, and we had to stay indoors. We headed back to Taiz the next day. No-one mentioned my passport again, it was as if I had never had it. There seemed to be nothing I could do or say to speed things up.

When we got back to Taiz Abdul Walli showed me a piece of paper covered in Arabic writing, and told me that my divorce had come through and this was the official document. He immediately put the piece of paper back in his pocket. I was shocked.

'What divorce?' I asked.

'Yours, from Abdullah.'

'What do I need a divorce for,' I wanted to know, 'when I'm not even married to him?'

'You've been here long enough to know our customs. You need a document to prove that you are not married to him. When you are set free you will be able to go wherever you want. You will have a choice. You will either live here in Taiz with Marcus – and you won't have to marry again – or else you can leave Marcus and go back to England. The choice will be yours.'

I couldn't think of anything to say. Although I had known they were going to make me choose eventually, it was still a shock to be actually confronted with such stark options. Not only would I be leaving Marcus, I would be leaving Nadia as well. I think until then I had been playing tricks with my own mind, telling myself that one day I would get out in order to keep my sanity, when underneath I didn't imagine it would ever happen. At the same time I had faith that there would be a happy ending for us all. Now I could see that whatever happened it was going to end in pain.

Apparently the Yemeni government had suddenly decided that it had had enough of me. The Foreign Minister, Doctor Ala-Riyani, called in the British Ambassador and said that he wanted to sort it out as quickly as possible. Either Abdullah had to sign a permission slip allowing me to go home, or he had to divorce me.

I was puzzled as to how they could have persuaded Abdullah to agree to the divorce, knowing how Abdul Khada had forbidden it and how frightened he was of his father. There was a policeman who used to come in and out of Abdul Walli's house while we were there, to get things like water for the others outside. He seemed to have Abdul Walli's complete confidence. He was very friendly to Nadia and me and often told us things that were going on and rumours that were circulating. I asked him what he knew about the divorce. He told me that the police had put Abdullah in prison, about five hours' drive away from Taiz, with chains round his ankles, and forced him to sign the necessary divorce papers.

I asked Abdul Walli if it was true and he admitted that Abdullah had been locked up for a while, which was why he hadn't come to Sana'a with us. Apparently he had cried constantly in his cell, but still refused to divorce me at first because Abdul Khada forbade it.

One of the reasons Abdul Khada didn't want the divorce to happen was because of the trouble he would have finding another wife for Abdullah. He would have to pay a lot of money to get anyone else to marry his son now, probably more money than he could find. I don't suppose he wanted to lose face by letting me get the better of him by escaping from his family.

I don't know what happened to Abdullah after he was let out of prison. I never saw him again. I imagine he went back to Saudi Arabia or to Hockail.

'You will be able to go soon,' Abdul Walli assured me,

'but you must wait three months, to ensure that you are not pregnant.' Even at that stage they didn't want to run the risk of losing a Yemeni baby to a foreign woman. 'And you must leave Marcus with Nadia.'

'Will he be allowed to stay with her?' I asked.

'Yes, for a while, but he will have to go back to his grandparents eventually.'

I made Abdul Walli promise me that Nadia could stay in the city and wouldn't have to go back to Mokbana. He agreed.

I tried to block what I was doing out of my mind, but I could only do it some of the time. When I was holding Marcus, looking down at him, I couldn't stop myself from thinking how I was going to lose him and how he would be growing up without me. I felt safe and secure that Nadia would be there for him, and I just hoped that when they let Nadia out she would be able to bring him with her.

Nadia was quite strong about me going; she just kept saying, 'Do everything you can to get me over to England.' But she knew that she was going to have to wait for Mohammed's passport to come through, and Gowad was still refusing to sign the necessary papers.

At one stage I received a call from Mum saying that she had heard from Jim and that he had got into trouble for handing out my passport before it had been stamped by the Yemen authorities, and now they wanted to know where it was. I didn't know what was happening with the passport, I just had to trust Abdul Walli to do the right things for me.

I was still having trouble believing that I was really free of Abdullah, but I kept asking people if it was true and they all told me that it was, so gradually I got used to the idea. Once I had finally accepted that I was divorced I knew that I was on my way home.

Abdul Walli came to the flat to tell me that I would be leaving in two days, and that I should pack a suitcase and be ready to drive to Sana'a. He gave us a thousand rials to buy presents which I could take back to our family. We didn't need to be asked twice. We went out and bought expensive little bottles of famous perfumes for Mum and our sisters, and also a clock for Mum. I bought myself a few things like a sponge bag and clothes for the kids. We didn't spend all the money and Nadia kept what was left.

We had stopped wearing the clothes that we had left the village in by then. The fashion had changed from the cloaks and skirts to long black coats which buttoned all the way down the front, so we had been wearing them for some time. When I knew I was going home I went out to buy a more western, beige-coloured coat, so that I would be less conspicuous when I got to England. I was still wearing the trousers underneath it, and still keeping my hair covered.

Nadia seemed happy that I was getting away, and she seemed confident that she would be following soon. Mohammed was very optimistic when I talked to him.

'As soon as Dad sends over the papers they need,' he would say, 'I will bring Nadia and the children over to see you.' I felt quite confident that I could trust him at that stage, because he seemed to want to come to England very badly.

'If anything goes wrong with Mohammed's passport,' Nadia told me, 'you've got to do everything you can to get me out of here. Don't leave it too long.'

'I won't,' I assured her, 'I promise.'

After we had finished the shopping we went back to the flat and I started packing my suitcase. Abdul Walli warned me not to pack too much, just one suitcase and a handbag. My suitcase was very small and the presents took up most of the space. I still had the English clothes that I had come out in eight years earlier. I could never have thrown anything away that was a reminder of my old life.

We were going to be driving to Sana'a overnight to get to the airport early in the morning, so we went to Abdul

Walli's house in the afternoon. Nothing seemed real, it was like walking in a dream. I felt sure that at any moment I would wake up back in the village and have to get up to start the day's work.

We had dinner at the house, and Mum phoned to find out how things were going. She promised to be at the airport to meet me. 'The worst thing is having to leave Nadia behind,' I told her.

'Don't worry about Nadia,' she assured me. 'She'll be coming out after you.'

The Land Rover was waiting at the back of the house, and we slid out of the back door. Abdul Walli carried my case so that I could carry Marcus in my arms. Nadia and the children came out of the house with us to say goodbye. Mohammed had decided to come with us to see me off, and we had a policeman with us as well. Nadia was being very brave. I said goodbye to Nadia, kissed Haney and Tina, and handed Marcus over to her. He was awake and looking at me as I went, but he didn't cry.

'Everything will be all right,' Nadia said.

'I know,' was all I could think to answer as I got into the Land Rover and we drove off into the darkness. None of the men spoke to me on the journey. We arrived at the airport just before dawn and I started to cry.

There was only one direct flight a week to London, even though it was a big, modern airport. Seeing all the planes coming and going it finally hit me that I really was leaving Nadia, Marcus and the other kids.

We went inside and I had to stand and wait patiently while Abdul Walli and Mohammed walked all around the airport, talking to people and arranging things. What I didn't know was that Jim Halley was also there, having been seeing off a friend. He watched me from a distance, to see that things were going all right.

Eventually Abdul Walli called me over and we went through some glass doors to an area where they weighed the luggage. They took my suitcase and I went back into the main airport to wait in the canteen. After a few minutes an airport official came up with Abdul Walli and gave me a blue form. He told me to fill it in.

'What's it for?' I asked.

'Just fill it in quickly,' the man said. 'We need it straight away.'

The questions were straightforward. I filled it in and gave it back and the man disappeared. For half an hour nothing happened and I felt sure they had found another reason to delay my departure and to take me back to Taiz. Eventually he returned with my passport and Abdul Walli handed it to me.

'You've now got your exit visa stamped,' he told me, and wandered off again, leaving me on my own.

I don't know if Abdul Walli had been lying to me when he told me he was getting my passport stamped all those weeks before, or whether it was just a mistake, but I finally had it in my hands, and that was all that mattered. Every second that we were still in the airport I expected policemen to appear and grab me and take me back to the Land Rover. I couldn't swallow and I felt physically sick from the nervous tension. I was shaking inside with fear.

The loudspeakers announced the arrival of a flight to London and I knew it was mine. Abdul Walli reappeared and told me to come and sit by the exit to the plane. Mohammed was nowhere to be seen. I shook Abdul Walli's hand and said goodbye to him. Then I walked through to the departure lounge.

With Abdul Walli gone I was finally on my own, and I was scared. There was no-one to turn to if things went wrong now. As far as anyone else knew I was just an Arab woman on my own. There were a lot of tourists and some Yemeni people sitting around waiting for the same plane.

'Is this the plane to London?' I asked the middle-aged American woman next to me, who seemed to be part of a group of people.

'Yes,' she smiled, 'where are you going?'

'I'm going back home to England.'

'Are you English?'

'Yes.'

'The way you were dressed I thought you must be a local, and you are so tanned.'

'I've been here eight years,' I explained.

'We've just been over here for three weeks, touring ... ' She chatted on and I was glad to have a friendly distraction from the tension. I could see officials arriving at the doors leading out to the tarmac, they were talking amongst themselves, and I was sure they were looking at me. ' ... We've been all over the Yemen, I loved it. I got some great shots in the cities, they are so old, I couldn't believe ... ' I was glad she wasn't asking me questions about myself, I was so tense I know I would have become aggressive if she had. Listening to her she sounded so free, able to go anywhere she wanted and do whatever she wanted.

They told us to come out to the plane. Two armed policemen stood at the door and we all had to file past, showing them our tickets. The first one looked into my handbag, then looked at my ticket. He nodded and I went to follow the other passengers through to the waiting bus.

'Hey!' he shouted after me. My heart was pounding in my ears and he signalled me to come back. 'Passport!' he snapped. I gave it to him and he thumbed slowly and deliberately through it, looking up at me as he did so.

'What do you want with my passport?' I asked, my voice trembling. 'Everyone else just showed you their ticket.' He said nothing, just kept staring. 'You obviously recognise who I am, and I'm going home,' I said. He narrowed his eyes and was about to speak.

'Let her through and give her back the passport,' his colleague shouted at him. The man seemed to swallow his protests and pushed the passport into my hands. I walked through to the bus. Everyone else was already on board, waiting for me; all their eyes seemed to follow me.

As I walked up the airplane steps I couldn't believe I was there. It still didn't seem possible that I was doing it.

It was only a small plane but I had a pair of seats to myself. I stared out of the window at the airport building. The plane began to move slowly across the tarmac and I kept expecting the door to open and somebody to leap in and pull me off at the last minute. As it gathered speed I felt the excitement building inside me and we lifted off into the air. The air hostess came and asked if I wanted anything to eat because it was Ramadan and most of the Yemenis were fasting at the time. I told her I wasn't hungry, but I made it clear that I wasn't fasting.

She went on down the plane and I looked back out the window at the Yemen landscape disappearing beneath the wings of the plane, growing smaller and smaller as we headed up into the clear blue skies, and I began to cry.

After a short flight we were going to have to stop at another Middle Eastern airport to let some people off and take on more. I began to imagine that they would take me off there and send me back. We landed but they told us we could stay on the plane, we didn't have to go into the airport building. I was relieved about that, but nothing seemed to be happening. I was watching out of the window when I saw a police van driving out over the tarmac towards us. My heart began to race again. The van stopped beneath our plane and two huge armed policemen clambered on board. They came over to my seat. They were staring straight at me, and then they walked on down the plane. They walked to the back and then came back up the aisle again. I kept looking at the floor, like a modest Arab woman, praying that they would just keep walking past me. They did, and got off the plane.

I heard people talking round me and they were saying that there were some escaped Palestinian terrorists in the area and they were checking all the planes that landed. We remained on the tarmac for over two hours before we finally took off for London.

CHAPTER NINETEEN

Back To England And Celebrity

I was like a sleepwalker when I got off the plane at London's Gatwick airport. I followed the rest of the passengers across the tarmac to the building. I was looking all around for my Mum, I felt scared. I could see people dressed in western clothes and I knew that I could have taken the scarf off my head and been as free as before I left England, but I couldn't do it, I was too much of a Yemeni woman.

We walked up some stairs and I noticed a woman at the top dressed in uniform. She was holding a piece of paper. She was looking at everyone who walked past.

'Zana?' she called out as I passed.

'Yeah,' I said, 'that's me.'

'I never would have recognised you.' She showed me the piece of paper she was holding which had an old photo of me. 'Don't worry, we have to take you a different way to the others because there is a pack of reporters outside waiting for you.'

I followed her down some corridors and she chatted to me in a friendly way. We collected my suitcase and she took it through customs for me. We went through another door and came back out onto the tarmac.

'This is for us.' She gestured to a waiting minibus. 'This will take you to your Mum.' We climbed in and started driving across the runway, past the planes all being checked and refuelled. A pair of police cars with flashing lights drove along on either side of us. The woman explained to me that there were television news crews all over the airport looking for me.

'You obviously don't want to face all that after what you've been through,' she said.

'No,' I agreed gratefully. 'I just want my Mum.'

I noticed a helicopter parked at the far side of the runway and we seemed to be heading straight towards it. As we got closer I saw that Mum was standing beside it. Then I recognised Eileen and Ben with her. The pilot was sitting inside the helicopter. The minibus stopped and we climbed out.

'Here's your daughter, Miriam,' the woman said. She climbed back into the bus and drove off with a wave.

I ran up to Mum and hugged her for ages. 'I can't believe I'm here,' was all I could think to say. She was crying and laughing and I was aware of the clicking of a camera as Ben circled round us taking pictures, but I didn't care. I had all I wanted at that moment.

'We've got to get in the helicopter to get out of the airport,' Mum said. 'It's the only way to get past the reporters. Eileen's arranged it.'

I was terrified – I had never been in a helicopter before – but I climbed in as I was told. 'Don't worry,' Mum said, but I could see she was frightened as well. As we lifted off the ground it wobbled from side to side and I was sure it was going to crash, but the pilot didn't seem bothered.

Eileen and Ben had climbed in too. 'How are you Zana?' she asked. 'How was your journey?'

'Fine,' I said, and then turned to Mum. 'I was scared Mum, I felt so alone in the plane.'

She nodded as if to say 'Don't worry, I'm with you now'.

'How's Nadia and the kids?' she asked.

'Fine.' I felt brave enough to look outside now at the Sussex countryside rushing beneath us. It all looked so green and fertile. After a short flight we landed in a field next to a house in the middle of nowhere. We climbed out, ducking under the roaring blades, the wind whipping at our clothes, and walked across the field to a country lane on the other side, where a car with a driver was waiting for us. Behind us the helicopter lifted back up and disappeared over the trees, leaving a deep silence behind it.

'Where are we going?' I asked.

'We're going to a hotel in Brighton,' Eileen told me as we climbed into the car.

The Grand Hotel was newly refurbished after the bomb which had nearly killed the British Government a few years before, but I didn't know anything about that at the time. All I saw was an expensive-looking, luxury hotel overlooking the sea. We must have been booked in already because Eileen gave Mum a key and told her how to get to the room, while she went to the desk to tell them we were there.

'When am I going home Mum?' was all I kept asking. I didn't want to stay there, I just wanted to get to see my brother and sisters and my friends.

'I don't know,' she shrugged, 'tomorrow maybe.'

'Why? I want to go now.'

'It's the reporters,' she explained. 'We have to stay out of their way for a while. They are waiting for us back home as well. If we go out now they will all be following and we don't want to go on telly just yet. You have to trust Eileen, she knows what she is doing.'

I didn't understand anything about newspapers then, but I thought probably Eileen wanted to keep the story for herself. After all she had done for us I thought she deserved that so I listened to Mum and kept quiet for a while. I felt very tired, too tired to eat or sleep that day. The last thing I wanted to do was appear on television, I felt much too shy and nervous for that. I still didn't realise just what was involved with the media, and Mum gradually explained to me just how much attention we were likely to be subjected to.

209

'I don't want to answer anyone's questions today,' I told them. 'I just want to be left alone.' They all understood. I felt like I didn't want to think about anything else until I had got Nadia back. I felt like I had left a part of me behind in the Yemen. I was trying to think all the time how to say the right things so that the Yemeni Government would allow Nadia and the kids out. I was so tired that everything was confused in my mind. I half felt that I wanted to get back to Nadia and the kids, and at one stage that day I said something about it. Mum must have been under a lot of pressure too, and she snapped when she heard me saying that. I guess she thought I wasn't grateful for everything she had done to get me out. She accused me of wanting to go back because I was in love with Abdul Walli. It was a silly thing for her to say, and she apologised afterwards, but it was too late because Eileen had overheard and thought she meant it. She became convinced that I was planning to go back to the Yemen to marry Abdul Walli. I was too confused that day to realise what impression we were making and the misunderstanding didn't show until Eileen started writing more in-depth stories later on.

Ben asked if we would go outside so that he could take some pictures. It was only April and it was really cold. I didn't want to but Mum said we would just do it quickly for him and then he would leave us alone. Mum and I went down on the beach with him for about twenty minutes. I was still wearing the headscarf, I couldn't quite pluck up the courage to take it off. I would have felt naked without it.

The next day we stayed in the hotel room. A couple of Eileen's friends from the *Observer* came to see us. They were very nice and they could see how upset I was so they didn't ask me any questions. Later in the day Eileen came up to warn us that some reporters from another paper had found out where we were staying and were downstairs. She told us that she had arranged for us to

210

move to another hotel, but we would have to slip out through a side door.

We followed her downstairs to a side door where there was a taxi waiting to drive us to London, to the Metropolitan Hotel. It was a much nicer place than the Grand, much more comfortable and not so posh. We stayed in the room all day and by the evening I had had enough.

'If they don't take me home now,' I said to Mum, 'I'm going on my own.'

'All right,' she said, 'we'll go. I'll talk to Eileen.'

She told Eileen how impatient I was getting, and how aggressive I was becoming. She came to see me.

'What is going on?' I demanded. 'I just want to go home.'

'OK,' she agreed, 'I'll organise a car and we'll go tomorrow.'

I slept well that night. The next morning Ben drove us up to Birmingham, and I felt able to put on some English clothes which Mum had brought down for me to wear. I don't remember much about the journey, I wasn't really aware of what was going on around me. I just wanted to get to my family. I could hardly sit still I was so impatient.

As we approached Birmingham city centre I saw the Rotunda building coming towards us, everything looked just as I remembered it and tears came to my eyes.

'Do you remember it?' Mum asked.

'Oh yes,' my voice cracked as I spoke. 'Where are we going now?'

'We're going to Mrs Wellington's house,' she explained. The thought of seeing the Wellingtons again, Lynny and her mother, was wonderful. I couldn't believe that it was finally happening. I remembered how Lynny and I used to help Mrs Wellington in her shop on a Sunday, serving behind the counter, and how she would give us pocket money to go to the pictures in the evening. They were wonderful friends to me.

211

Mrs Wellington has a house in Sparkbrook, and as we came into the area I was staring out of the window like a child, trying to spot some of my old friends on the street. Mum was watching me with a smile on her face.

'What are you thinking?' she asked.

'I can't wait to see all the family.'

When we drew up outside the house I climbed out of the car and our whole family came spilling out of the front door. Mo, Ashia, Tina, and Ashia's daughter Lana who I had never seen before. Mrs Wellington came out with her two elder daughters. As I got closer I could see that they were all crying. Lynny had a flat of her own down the road and she had been told I was there and was on her way.

We went into the house and sat on the sofa, everybody went quiet. Ashia was crying the most, and Tina had changed so much in the eight years that I didn't recognise her; she had grown so tall. All I could think about was Nadia still stuck out in the Yemen. It gave me a lump in my throat and I wasn't able to talk. Eileen and Ben were there and then Lynny arrived. I recognised her immediately, although she was a grown-up woman now. She was much prettier than she had been as a girl, with a short hair cut, she had grown much taller too. We hugged each other and cried and neither of us could find any words to say. She just kept staring at me and crying and shaking her head in amazement that I was actually back.

'You've changed, you've changed,' was all she could say. 'You're so tanned.'

Mum and I stayed with the Wellingtons for four days and the others went back to Mum's house and came down each day. Ben and Eileen stayed at a hotel in Birmingham and came out to see us each day. I think they were staying around to make sure no other papers got to us. Just before they left Ben took a whole lot of pictures of us all in the garden. I didn't want him and Eileen around any more, they were beginning to depress me.

'I don't want any more photographs,' I told Mum.

'We need these pictures for the publicity,' she said, 'to

help Nadia.' So I kept quiet for a bit longer.

After four days I was ready to move back to Mum's house in King's Heath, where she had moved when she left Dad. Mum and I took a taxi up there and everyone else waited in for us to arrive. It was a small house, but it felt so cosy and comfortable to be back amongst my family.

For a few weeks reporters would come to the door now and again and ask for me, but I wouldn't see them. The others would answer the door and send them away. Some of them were hanging around outside, so I couldn't go anywhere for a while. I couldn't face them on the street. The only place I went in the first couple of weeks was down to Lynny's flat or Mrs Wellington's house. Ashia used to take me down in a taxi.

Tom Quirke, the journalist from the *Birmingham Post* got back in contact with Mum to find out what was happening to Nadia. We started to go down to his office and use the phones to call Abdul Walli's house in Taiz. We were able to talk quite regularly, so I knew she was still in the city and that Marcus was all right. She and Mohammed both told me not to worry, that as soon as the papers came through they would be following me out. He was still waiting for Gowad to send the papers. I understood that a lot of reporters were going to Gowad's house in Birmingham to find out what was happening, but he was refusing to answer the door or speak to anyone.

Whatever assurances they gave me, I always went back to worrying, because I knew how easily things could just drift on out there, and how people would never keep their promises. I couldn't settle down to thinking about straightening my own life out as long as Nadia was still trapped out there with the kids.

The only other person who could help Nadia was Dad. If he had said that his daughter and grandchildren were unhappy over there, he could demand that they be allowed to come back to this country and I know Gowad wouldn't have argued with him. But he wouldn't help.

213

'I need to go and see Dad,' I told Mum, 'to try to get him to help get Nadia out.'

I dressed myself up as a Yemeni again for the visit, with the trousers and scarf, wanting to show him how I had changed and how I was a respectful daughter now. I took a taxi down to the café on my own. The café looked the same. I paid off the taxi and walked in. I saw him behind the counter and felt nothing.

'Zana!' he exclaimed, and started to cry. I didn't cry. I walked through to the back and waited for him. Once the customers had gone out he closed up and came through. He was still crying and couldn't find the words.

'I'm sorry for what happened,' he said. 'If I had known earlier how you were being treated out there things would have been different.' I knew he was lying because all the Yemeni people I had spoken to who had travelled back and forth to England over the years had told him what was going on, and we had written all those letters to him, telling him how miserable we were. I didn't want to go over all that again, I just wanted to get his help with Nadia.

'Well I'm back now,' I said, 'and as you can see I'm still a Muslim and respectful of you. I love you Dad and I want your help with getting Nadia and her husband out so that we can live as one big happy family again.'

He nodded, accepting everything I said. 'I will go and talk to Gowad,' he promised. 'You have experienced the proper life now, you can speak Arabic and you have a better understanding of life. That is all I wanted for you.'

'Yes, I am more mature now,' I agreed. 'So you'll go and see Gowad about Nadia?'

'Yes I will. You can come to see him too.' I believed that he meant what he said because he made an arrangement for us to meet Gowad.

I dressed up in the Arab clothes again and went down to Gowad's house at the appointed time. It was a big old house. I saw Salama. I spoke to her but I felt hatred towards her because of what she had done to Nadia at

214

the end. She was still dressed like a village woman, and she had a new two-year-old daughter.

'Why did you leave us to struggle with your children all that time?' I asked. 'We wanted to know what was going on, nobody ever told us. Why did you do it?'

'I'm going back soon,' she promised, 'and Nadia and Mohammed are coming over with the children.'

'Yes I know they are.' I didn't bother to say any more, I knew I was wasting my breath. I was still managing to stay polite, but I could feel the aggression building up inside me again and I didn't want to let it out in case I made them angry and spoilt Nadia's chances.

Dad spoke to Gowad in Arabic, but I could follow what they were saying now. Gowad promised to do everything he could. 'It takes time,' he said, 'but they will come.'

Nothing ever happened. I don't believe they ever meant to do anything in the first place, they just wanted to quieten me down.

I heard rumours from Arab travellers passing through Birmingham that Nadia had gone back to the village with the children. They would recognise me in the street and stop me and tell me what was happening. They said she went willingly, but I know that can't be true.

Ahmed came over to visit us as well, and he had heard the same stories. He told us that Leilah was very ill and needed to come to England for medical tretment. Mum got her birth certificate and Ahmed said he would take it back to Aden with him.

A few months later there was a knock on the front door and my brother, Mo, told me Leilah had arrived. I went out into the street and I saw her for the first time, sitting in a mini-bus outside with her husband. She looked like Nadia. The four children were asleep in the van. She got out and she was crying, but all I could think was, why can you escape when Nadia can't?

She looked ill. It was cold and she and Mum just

215

hugged on the pavement, not wanting to let each other go. I wanted to get her inside in the warm as quickly as possible. We took them in with all their luggage and they stayed in the house for a few days while we arranged for Leilah to see the local doctor. Mum had kept her medical card from when she was a baby, so all she had to do was renew it. Once she was better they moved into a rented house.

According to rumour Nadia has had another baby. If that is true she must have left Taiz and not been able to get contraception any more. There was no chance that she would have wanted to have another child after all the trouble she had had with Tina's birth, and with all the work of looking after her, Haney, Marcus and probably Salama's two children as well.

I tried telephoning Abdul Walli to ask why he had broken his word to me and not kept Nadia in the city, but he was never there to take my calls any more. Mum rang Jim in Sana'a but he said he didn't know anything about what was happening. The lines of communication had been cut again, and Nadia had slipped out of our reach. We went back to waiting and hoping.

My experiences have made me more aware of what is happening in the world. Now, when I watch programmes on television about homeless children and families being split up, I hurt so much I could burst.

CHAPTER TWENTY

Creating An International Incident

It took me at least a year to find my feet in England. Freedom can be a frightening thing when you are not used to it, when you are used to having other people make all your decisions for you, when you have no choices to make. I couldn't think straight, all the time my mind was on Nadia and Marcus, and I cried until I had no more tears left. I felt so helpless and so far away from them.

Before I had left for the Yemen, all those years ago, when I was still just an innocent schoolgirl, I had had a boyfriend called Jimmy. He was a sweet boy, a good friend. I had often thought of him while I was trapped in the mountains, and wondered how he was getting on. I knew that he was in love with me, but I hadn't really imagined what it would be like to see him again after so long. But there he was, still in all the same places as before I went away, like nothing had happened.

'Look,' he said when I saw him, 'I never forgot you.' He pulled out his wallet and showed me a picture of myself, a young girl with no idea of what lay ahead.

He had never stopped loving me, and he was just as kind and funny and gentle as I remembered. It felt good for me to have him there again. He was living at home

217

with his family, so when things become too tense and crowded round at Mum's I would go and stay with Jimmy, and they made me feel like one of the family.

After a year I realised that nothing was going to happen about Nadia unless we made it happen. Mum had been doing the best she could, banging on every door imaginable, talking to advice centres and solicitors and wrecking her health trying to find a way round the problem. Everyone was sympathetic, but no one knew what to do. I decided that I should write a book. I felt that if I could do that I would have something which I could use to publicise Nadia's plight. I could talk to journalists and television people – even though the thought of it terrified me – and put our side of the story in full. But I knew I needed help with the writing. A friend went to the library and asked for the name of a ghostwriter who could help and I was given the number of Andrew Crofts.

Getting a book written and published is a long, slow business, but I was used to waiting. After all those years I knew how to be patient. Andrew produced a synopsis and his agent found us a British publisher, and then I had to relive the whole horrible story again. All the details which I had been suppressing and trying to forget had to come out again and I had to cope with it. It took me nearly three days to tell Andrew the story from start to finish and many of the memories made me cry all over again.

Then it went quiet once more as we waited for the first edition of the book to come out, and I fell pregnant. I loved my pregnancy and I received wonderful support from Jimmy and his family. I desperately wanted to have this baby, someone who would be completely my own, someone that no one else could take away from me.

All the time I knew in my heart what had happened to Nadia, that by now she would be back in the village, probably pregnant again herself, and lost in the endless drudgery of serving the men, children and old women.

Some days I would become frantic with the frustration of being so helpless. I went again to see my Dad, because I knew that with a word from him and from Gowad everything would be changed, but I got nowhere. He said he would help, but I knew he wouldn't. Mum had found a solicitor, called Kate, who said she thought we had a chance of accusing them of false imprisonment and kidnapping, and of getting Dad and Gowad into court. We decided to try it.

There was one appearance in court, but the case was adjourned due to insufficient evidence, and we all went back to waiting while the wheels of the law ground slowly forwards and we collected proof from Islamic experts, friends and family.

Liam was born in November 1990 and he was wonderful. I was still living with Mum but I applied for a flat on my own to try to give him a bit more space. Ayshea and her kids were at Mum's as well and there simply wasn't room for us all any more.

Our case was handed on to another solicitor, Madeleine, and we were advised not to undergo too much publicity for the book when it came out as it might jeopardise the case. We did what they said and although the book sold out there was very little fuss or publicity, which had been the point of doing it in the first place. I had been booked to do all sorts of interviews, including *Wogan*, which was the biggest chat show at the time, but we cancelled it all on the advice of the solicitors. We put all our faith in them, but they did not move any further on and the months continued to pass. It was like trying to push a giant rock up a steep mountain. Nothing seemed to offer us any hope and we were getting so tired.

Then the literary agent began to sell foreign rights to the book, all over Europe. Before long it was being translated into about sixteen different languages, and after years of waiting, things began to happen. There was nothing to stop us from publicising our story outside England, and journalists from all the other countries were hungry for details. The German publishers brought reporters to England to meet me, and then the French publishers, Fixot, made a suggestion.

The book *Not Without My Daughter* had been an enormous success in Paris, selling more copies than any other book in years and making the author, Betty Mahmoody, a national celebrity. She is an American who married an Iranian and went to visit Iran with him and their daughter. Her husband's family then turned against her and would not let her leave with the child, making them both prisoners. The book is all about how they managed to escape and it was made into a film with Sally Field playing Betty. Fixot were Betty's publishers in France and they suggested that she should write a foreword for the French edition of my book, and help us to promote it. I will always agree to anything that might help to spread the story further and am always grateful for help from anyone.

The first time they invited me to Paris I wasn't expecting anything more than what had happened with the media in Britain in the past. I went with Mum and Liam and we agreed to stay for a week while the book was being launched. It was called *Vendues!* and they had done a great job on translating and producing it. Nothing had prepared me for the barrage of interviews which were lined up, one after another, from morning to night. Liam became like a permanent fixture in the publishers' offices and Susanna Lea, an English girl who worked for them, was assigned to look after me. She and her colleague Antoine took us everywhere, translating for us and smoothing our path round Paris.

But this was the first time I had had to relive the years in the Yemen in detail since talking to Andrew Crofts two years before, and this time I was having to go over it time and again. My spirits were sinking. I felt overwhelmed with depression as all the memories rose back up again and there still seemed no hope of getting Nadia back. Betty Mahmoody appeared with me on

220

some of the interviews, telling her side of the story. She was obviously a brave woman, but her personal ordeal was over now, her daughter safely back in America, while our nightmare continued. Whenever we had some spare hours Mum and I would go sightseeing, and people started to recognise me in the street. I could see them nudging one another and whispering my name. All of them smiled sympathetically.

One of the interviews was on a live television chat show called *Sacrée Soirée*, which is one of the most popular programmes in France, hosted by a man called Jean-Pierre Foucault. We were taken to the studios in a taxi and Susanna explained, as she always did, who the other guests on the show would be and what was expected of me. I think they were all as nervous as I was, frightened that I would say the wrong things and embarrass myself.

When we reached the studios I had my own dressing room with my name on the door, champagne and canapés inside and light bulbs all round the mirror, just like in the movies. I was taken to make-up and my nerves grew tighter.

There was a live audience in the studio, as well as the millions watching at home. Waiting behind the scenes for my cue was agonising, then I heard my name and walked out to the chairs. The heat from the spotlights was massive. Concentrating on what the interpreters were saying took my mind off my fear and as the interview progressed I felt confident and fluent. Afterwards they all told me I had done well, but I don't think any of us quite realised what an impact the show had had on the public, or what it was going to lead to.

Mum and I went home to England and my depression overwhelmed me. It all seemed so hopeless. We had done all that and still we were no further on. We still didn't know what was happening to Nadia or how we would get to her.

For two weeks there was silence. By now Jimmy and I

had split up. It was my fault. It was impossible for me to put any effort into a relationship when all I thought about was Nadia. I was terrible to live with and I wasn't ready for a serious relationship. Having Liam was a Godsend, giving some purpose to my daily routine, and Jimmy and his family continued to be my best friends and supporters. I was offered a flat by a housing association and took it, happy to get some privacy for Liam and me, but lonely and scared at the same time.

Two weeks after returning from Paris, Susanna rang me. 'The media have gone mad,' she said, 'and the public are bombarding the Yemeni embassy with mail. There are articles everywhere. Bernard can't sleep for thinking about Nadia and he wants to do something to help, not just to sell more copies of the book, but to actually get Nadia out.'

Bernard Fixot was the boss of the publishers. He is a great cuddly bear of a man who I had met on my first trip and who had cried openly at my story. His wife is the daughter of Giscard d'Estaing, the former President of France. At last some truly powerful people were taking an active interest in our problems.

'You have been invited back on to *Sacrée Soirée*,' Susanna told me, 'and this time there will be someone there from the Yemeni embassy.'

This was good news. At last I would be able to confront the Yemeni authorities in public. The man the embassy sent was referred to as Mr Shoki. The Ambassador, I was told later, had been keen to let Nadia and the children out immediately to save any further embarrassment, but Mr Shoki had persuaded him otherwise, and was willing to defend his position in public. He was tenser than I was as we waited for the show to begin, but I was angrier. I had truth on my side and that made me brave. Once we were out under the lights he kept repeating phrases like 'Nadia is a Yemeni citizen' and 'she is happy, she doesn't want to come out'. He was sweating and panicking and I was going at him with all my energy. He could tell the audience was against him as he contradicted himself and tried to deny things that were obvious. The audience were letting our hissing noises when he spoke and the atmosphere became more and more tense as he became more deeply enmeshed in the official lies.

I was in a fury by the time Jean-Pierre Foucault interrupted to tell me that they had Nadia on the telephone, and asked if I wanted to speak to her. It was as if the breath had been knocked out of me. I couldn't believe it was true. I hadn't been able to contact her in four years and now I could speak to her in front of millions of television viewers? How could this be possible?

I took the microphone from Jean-Pierre in a trance. 'Hello?' I spoke as if to some invisible ghost.

There was a crackling over my headphones and I heard Nadia's voice – 'Hello!'

The tears poured down my cheeks as I tried to get her to hear me and to communicate across the air, but we didn't seem able to get together, floundering in different parts of the world, both shocked and puzzled. Jean-Pierre wound up the show and I was taken to a small room where the telephone reception was clearer. We were through.

'What's going on?' Nadia wanted to know, 'what are you doing?'

I started to explain, but all the things that had happened in the last four years came tumbling to the front of my brain at once and the words were falling over one another – and then the line went dead. I was stunned and heartbroken. To make such a fleeting contact and then to have it broken was almost too cruel to bear.

On the show Jean-Pierre had challenged Mr Shoki: 'Why can't Nadia see her family?' He had been given the usual, snake-like evasions of the truth, but he hadn't let it drop. 'Then we will take Zana and her mother into the Yemen for a meeting with her.' His words had been

223

eclipsed by the phone call, but now they were coming back to me in all their horror. They were planning to take me back to the Yemen! The thought was terrifying. Supposing they didn't let me out again, and I was trapped once more?

As we came out of the phone room I heard Mr Shoki talking to the embassy on the phone. He was speaking in Arabic. 'Let them go over,' he hissed, 'they can't prove anything. It will help us show how things are.'

It was all getting beyond my control. I was frightened. 'I don't want to do it,' I told Mum.

'We've got to try, Zana,' she said, 'we've got to let her know what's going on, that she's not on her own, that we're still fighting to get her out.'

I agreed, but I was still quaking at the thought of leaving Liam and putting myself in such danger. Suddenly the Yemeni government was all smiles. They told us we could see Nadia and her children for as long as we wished, and I would be able to see Marcus.

'And if you want to take Marcus out of the country,' they told me kindly, 'you can make an application to the courts.' I knew I shouldn't believe a single word of it, but when you are drowning you will clutch at anything.

Jean-Pierre knew I was frightened. 'Don't worry,' he said, 'if they try to kidnap you I will be your ransom.'

Bernard and Madame Fixot were convinced that they had made a big step forward, and said they would be coming down with us. A private, ten-seater plane was arranged. Our party included Mum and me, Bernard and his wife, Jean-Pierre, a camera man and his assistant, and Mr Shoki, who was taking the opportunity of a free flight to visit his friends and family.

The night before Mum and I stayed with Bernard and his wife in Paris. They have a beautiful home, like a converted warehouse, where they live with two Polish children they have adopted. Bernard was so optimistic, and I kept telling him that he would have to see for himself before he would believe how hard it was going to be to get anything done.

We landed first in Sana'a, and outside the airport were at least thirty official-looking Yemeni men, all waiting for us. There was also a local film crew. They took our passports and Mr Shoki disappeared off with his colleagues. Everyone was busy whispering and arguing, leaving Mum and me sitting alone. All my memories of the smells of the place came back, making me shiver in anticipation of what might be to come. After a while they moved us to the Sheraton Hotel and told us that in the morning we would go to Taiz, and there we would meet Nadia.

The plane was ready early the next morning and we flew down. As we were driven into the city centre, they told us that we would be able to meet in a private room and talk for as long as we wanted. My heart was beating in my ears and I found it hard to get my breath. I hardly dared to believe that they were actually going to keep their word and let us meet.

We arrived at a government building and we were shown into a garden, where we waited once again. All around the garden, keeping a respectful distance, were thirty or forty Yemeni men, probably the same ones who had been waiting for us at the airport. Some of them had video cameras. We sat there for two hours.

'They will be briefing Nadia on what to say,' I told Bernard.

Nadia appeared at the entrance to the garden, swathed from head to foot in black. The cameras started to whirr on all sides as she made her way towards us. She had her husband Mohammed with her, and their youngest child. Her face was thin and drawn and she had white patches of pigmentation on her skin. Her eyes darted from side to side, confused and frightened. The crowd kept their distance, watching silently.

She stopped a few feet in front of us and held her hands out. 'What's going on?' she asked me. Her voice trembled with fear.

I started talking and just let it all pour out. For half an hour we sat together in the garden as I tried to tell her as much as possible. Mohammed hovered nervously around us, casting anxious glances at the men who watched. The cameras kept going and Jean-Pierre stepped forward to do his interview. With the cameras on her she covered her face, her eyes wide with fear as she started to spout the lines which they had taught her.

'I am a Muslim. I am happy here. I would like to visit England with my husband and children, but without the fuss. If the media stop their attentions we can come.'

'The media took no notice for four years,' Mum interrupted, unable to contain herself, 'if the spotlight is turned off now things will go back to the beginning and nothing will happen.'

'We will never give up trying to get you out,' I insisted. It was like talking to someone in a daze. I wanted to shake her and bring her to her senses. She might be nearly thirty now, but she had never had a chance to develop beyond the frightened fourteen year old who was first imprisoned. This was still my baby sister and I felt powerless to save her.

Mohammed was becoming frantic with nerves, saying that they had to get back to the other children in the village. He must have been under a lot of pressure.

'Where's Marcus?' I wanted to know.

'His grandfather would not allow him to come,' an official told me, and I remembered the spite and tyranny with which Abdul Khada used to rule his family, and I felt sick with sadness for my lost son.

'They said I could see him.' I was so angry I couldn't even cry. 'They said that if I wanted him I could fight for him in the courts here.'

The officials shrugged, exchanging glances and hiding their amused smiles badly. 'There is no way for you to do that,' they told me, and I felt my rage building. In a way I was angry with myself for letting them build my hopes up, even that small amount. I should know by now that

226

government officials will say whatever suits them at that moment, whatever country they come from. I am resigned now to the fact that I will probably not see Marcus again until he is grown-up enough to make his own decisions. All I have is one picture of him as a baby which I keep in the flat and show to Liam. I have no idea what he looks like now.

Mohammed agreed to let Nadia come in the jeep with Mum and me for the ten minute ride to a hotel where we were to rest until flying out. Once in the privacy of the car Nadia opened up a little and asked after Jimmy and other friends. We showed her some photos we had brought with us. She began to cry softly. 'I would like to come back,' she whispered, 'and they say I can leave with you now, but I cannot take the children. I can't leave them. I can't endanger their lives. The men are threatening me all the time, telling me what I must say. I just want to be left alone.'

Mum and I were dropped at the hotel and Mohammed took Nadia away. It was all over, just like that, and nothing had changed. Nadia was going straight back to the village and Mum and I waited at the hotel for several hours while the others in our party drove around Taiz sightseeing and taking background film. But film of the city wouldn't show people the way that Nadia was having to live in the village. I had told them that and they had asked if we could go out to the Mokbana.

'No, no, no,' the officials had shaken their heads and given sharp intakes of breath, 'too dangerous, much too dangerous . . . bandits . . . bad men.'

Now Mum and I were waiting again, watched by silent eyes. Every sudden noise made me jump, every man's voice made me shiver inside. I did not relax until we were back on the plane, heading for Paris and the television studio, to show the public what had happened.

Mr Shoki was triumphant. Nadia had repeated all the phrases that they wanted. 'You can see for yourselves . . .' he crowed, 'just listen to her.'

227

But the audience saw the hurt in Nadia's eyes as she spoke and they hissed him again. The press weren't fooled either and the next day they were full of the sadness of the sights they had seen through the camera. In their eyes my sister was still a little girl, being held against her will as her life ebbed away from her in an endless grind of toil and repression.

Bernard was obviously dispirited by what had happened, but he swore to me that he would never give up.

The book was now coming out all over the world and I travelled to Amsterdam, Brussels, Rome and Milan to give endless strings of interviews. Letters come every day now to Birmingham from every country where the book is published, expressing sympathy and support – but still nothing has changed.

Jean-Pierre made the authorities promise to let us in to see Nadia whenever we wanted, but I heard after our return that there had been factions who had wanted to snatch me while I was in the country, and I can't risk that. Mum has been back again, with a friend. They stayed at a hotel in Taiz for three and a half months and saw Nadia only twice. She was pregnant again and delivered another baby while Mum was in the country. A doctor told Mum that the next baby could easily kill her. Mum and her friend were harassed and attacked by men in the street, accused of being trouble makers, followed wherever they went and their room was bugged.

We asked the Foreign Office for help, and we were assigned to a woman. We later heard that she had advised the Vice Consul in the Yemen that Mum was trouble and he should avoid her. He did the best he could to help anyway, but his hands were tied. Mum ran out of money half-way through her stay and I asked the woman at the Foreign Office to help me get some to her, but she refused.

'We tried to help you thirteen years ago,' she told me, 'but you wouldn't accept our help. We can't do any more now.'

I remember that time very clearly. I doubt if I will ever forget it, and no one tried to help us. One month we get a letter from the Foreign Office saying there is nothing they can do because Nadia is a dual-national. The next month we get an apology and a denial that this is the case. No one seems to know anything for sure.

Helena Kennedy, a well-known lawyer in England, showed an interest in our case, saying she wanted to take it up for personal reasons, but the years have passed and her latest advice was that we should drop our charges against Gowad.

So we are still waiting. We constantly hear rumours of some fresh hope, but they are always dashed or just peter out to nothing except more waiting. We won't give up until we get Nadia back. There has to be someone out there who can help us, and we'll keep going till we find them.